A Woman's

Voice

~ Inspirational Short Stories ~

Volumes 1, 2 & 3

DOLORES AYOTTE

A Woman's Voice (Inspirational Short Stories) Combined Set ~ Volume 1, 2, & 3
Copyright © 2014 by Dolores Ayotte. All rights reserved.

No part of this publication may be reproduced, stored in a retrieval system or transmitted in any way by any means, electronic, mechanical, photocopy, recording or otherwise without the prior permission of the author except as provided by Canada and United States copyright law.

Book design copyright © 2014 by Dolores Ayotte. All rights reserved.
Cover design by Dolores Ayotte
Cover photo by Shirley Gauthier Sarafinchan
Interior design by Dolores Ayotte
Printed by CreateSpace
Published in Canada
ISBN: 978-0-9948673-4-6
Self-Help, Motivational & Inspirational

Disclaimer: The suggestions provided in this inspirational book are based on a personal point of view and not in any professional capacity.

Introduction

A Woman's Voice ~ Inspirational Short Stories Combined Set is the compilation of Volumes 1, 2 and 3. All three volumes have been combined for your convenience. I sincerely hope that you enjoy this series of short motivational stories and personal reflections. Please take a few moments whenever possible. Grab yourself a soothing beverage of your choice. Then imagine a dear friend sitting across the table or room from you in the comfort of your own home as we reminisce about the past, present, and what the future might hold. We may be shaped by the events that have taken place in our past; however, we can definitely alter our present situation and create boundless opportunities for change in our futures.

Live, Laugh, Love and Enjoy!

Dolores Ayotte

A Woman's Voice

~ Inspirational Short Stories ~

Volume 1

DOLORES AYOTTE

A Woman's Voice (Inspirational Short Stories) Volume 1
Copyright © 2012 by Dolores Ayotte. All rights reserved.

No part of this publication may be reproduced, stored in a retrieval system or transmitted in any way by any means, electronic, mechanical, photocopy, recording or otherwise without the prior permission of the author except as provided by Canada and United States copyright law.

Book design copyright © 2012 by Dolores Ayotte. All rights reserved.
Cover design by Dolores Ayotte
Cover photo by Shirley Gauthier Sarafinchan
Interior design by Dolores Ayotte
Printed by CreateSpace
Published in Canada
ISBN: 978-0-9948673-1-5
Self-Help, Motivational & Inspirational

Disclaimer: The suggestions provided in this inspirational book are based on a personal point of view and not in any professional capacity.

The Human & Humane Self-Help Author

Dolores holds a Bachelor of Arts degree with a major in psychology from the University of Winnipeg as well as teacher certification from the University of Manitoba. She has also taken courses in human relationships and communication.

Her self-help books are written in retrospect based on a proven recipe, one she has incorporated step by step into her own life. Over time, Dolores eventually developed better life coping skills which inspired her to put pen to paper and write three previous books about her experiences. She utilizes quotes, anecdotes, humor and her own personal stories when necessary to make her suggestions relevant and to give an example of how to use her simple tips in daily living.

She is now retired and spends half the year with her husband at a retirement community in Arizona. For the remainder of the year, Dolores enjoys her children and grandchildren in Winnipeg, Manitoba where she was born and raised. She continues to learn from all the people who touch her life.

Table of Contents

Introduction

1. The Empty Nest
2. Unconditional Love versus Conditional Love
3. The Big Copout
4. You Are Not Broken ~ Andrea Ayotte Cockerill
5. He's Got the Whole World in His Hands
6. The Jongleur
7. The Three R's
8. Confidence in God
9. First Things First
10. Psst…Hey Ewe!
11. The Absence Of
12. Love Triangle ~ Fred Ayotte
13. Positive Attitude
14. The Truth
15. On Being Judgmental
16. Connecting the Dots
17. Child's Play…or is it?
18. Found Money
19. Drip…Drop ~ A Christmas Thought
20. Christmas Love

Conclusion

Introduction

As I enter into my twilight years, I want to permanently shed my insecurities and enter this final stage of my life with as much grace and wisdom as humanly possible. I have been an observant student for the majority of my life. Perhaps now, after all these years, I can get into the driver's seat and call myself a good teacher. I have succeeded in learning to "teach without classroom walls" and I have now written my own motivational books to go along with this philosophy. This experience has been extremely liberating for me. I hope by reading what I have to say and by incorporating some of my suggestions into your life, you too can find a sense of true freedom and peace.

At the end of each chapter, there is an opportunity for personal reflection. I recommend that you take a moment to personally consider the questions posed and how my words can make a difference in your life. As you can see by this lovely cover, a photo generously provided by my talented sister Shirley Gauthier Sarafinchan, the reflection in the water can be seen as a gentle reminder that as life goes on we have many opportunities to live, learn, and reflect on life in general. We also have every opportunity to learn from these reflections to help ensure that history doesn't repeat itself.

There is no need to rush through this inspirational book. It is meant to be read slowly, pondered upon, used as a stepping stone to reflect upon its content, its message and how it applies to each of you in your own life. I also want you to realize that my voice is only a soft whisper. Please hear it this way. It's from my heart to yours. Maya Angelou's words mirror my exact sentiments. *"The idea is to write it so that people hear it and it slides through the brain and goes straight to the heart"*.

"When the wish for peace is genuine, the means for finding it is given in a form each mind that seeks for it in honesty can understand." ~ *Helen Schucman & William Thetford*

1 ~ The Empty Nest

The house is quiet as we both go about our usual business. We are never alone despite the silence that endures between us. This is a result of a true and unending love relationship that started as a friendship between my husband and me.

After over forty years of marriage, sharing a home, first only with each other…then raising a family, we sit in the peaceful silence of our empty nest knowing that this is our quiet time together. We have not entered our twilight years lightly nor without great thought and careful planning. We know that we are on the home stretch of, not only our years together, but of our very lives. We have more years to look back on than ahead. It is good…in fact, it is more than good, it is all that I could have ever dreamed of or hoped for in the life that has been given to me. I am forever grateful to have been given so much. I take nothing for granted and each day I thank God for my many blessings.

Some refer to this stage of life as the "empty nest" while I prefer to see it as the stage of life when we can sit back and be grateful for having survived its challenges. It is not an easy feat to simultaneously marry young, educate ourselves, and raise a family. We all go through the growing pains that must take place in order to accomplish and succeed in our efforts to have a successful marriage. Yet, I'm not so sure what appears to be a successful marriage is always a happy one…by that, I mean would you do it all over again if the choice was yours to make?

At this moment in time, I find myself more content and reflective. I not only have embraced this quiet time of my life, I have worked towards it. This opportunity leads to numerous seeds ready to germinate into the little stories I so deeply enjoy sharing. Not too long ago, one of my fellow authors suggested it would be a great book idea to write about the ingredients that make up a really good marriage, not a marriage that one endures but rather a holy union that one would eagerly say "yes" to again if they had to start all over.

Take a moment to just sit there and reflect. Think about the person you are married to and how you view him/her. Just between you and your Maker, would you honestly marry this person again? Be really honest now? Remember, if you can't be honest in this personal quiet time when you look at your spouse, it will be very difficult for you to be honest in your relationship. So…would you actually marry your spouse knowing all that you do today? I'm just asking for a simple 'yes or no'. No more, no less. I don't want to hear a maybe because it implies that you want your spouse to change. That's not what this is all about. Plain and simple…would you marry your spouse again if given a second chance to choose otherwise?

If the answer is a resounding no, then my next question is why? Is your spouse such a disappointment to you that if given a second chance you might say 'no' or 'maybe if'? Is it really about misplaced expectations or is it about not knowing what true love really is? A relative once stated that I had a perfect marriage. I would have to disagree. To have a perfect marriage implies perfection or a union of two perfect people. Most of us know full well that such a concept is absolutely impossible and does not exist, at least not on this side of the turf…but I do believe in perfect love. To me, perfect love is learning to love and accept your spouse no matter what. All you need to do is refer to those old-fashioned marriage vows to get my drift. Do you still believe in those words…if so, you are on the right track? All you need to do is visualize yourself riding off into the sunset with your better half. If you can do this…the sky's the limit.

"Love means the body, the soul, the life, the entire being. We feel love as we feel the warmth of our blood, we breathe love as we breathe the air, we hold it in ourselves as

we hold our thoughts. Nothing more exists for us." ~ *Guy De Maupassant*

"How you react towards your spouse is a choice rooted in your heart." ~ Jim Hughes

2 ~ Unconditional Love versus Conditional Love

A friend of mine has been having a difficult time the last couple of months. She has a married son. He is her only child and he also has one son, her only grandchild. They live several hundred miles apart; therefore, she doesn't see this precious little family very often. As a result, my friend has gotten to know her infant grandchild very well through the use of Skype and other means of communication with her son and daughter-in-law. However, the last time they came home to visit, there was an unfortunate turn of events and things did not go well. Now, the communication is no longer the same. There is no more Skyping and the emails are few and far between. She mentioned something that prompted me to write this article. She said that when they do communicate, that the "sign off" is now different. They don't always "sign off" with their name or they don't "sign off" with the word "love" anymore. I find this very odd.

I have also had the misfortune of unsmooth relationships in my life. How about you? Please bear with me as I ask a few more questions. Does anyone really know and understand the meaning of "**un**conditional love"? In actuality, "**un**conditional love" is just that…no conditions, whether tacit or verbal, when offering our love to others. It is what I refer to as "perfect love" or acceptance. We all know that there is no such thing as perfect people. If the love we have for others is based on the expectation of perfection or requires others to conform to our way of thinking, it is doomed to fail.

So I dare to ask, what kind of love do you offer? Loved based on conditions is really not love at all. In my opinion, it is kind of like a pseudo-love whereby it must be earned in order to receive it or we must behave in a certain manner in order to be worthy of it. When someone upsets us and we still need to communicate for whatever reason, it may be merely as simple as looking at how we now "sign off" in our communication with them after the altercation. Take a moment to think about it and you will know exactly what I mean. We really can be a lot more apparent than we realize.

It can be likened to child's play…I won't love you anymore if…I won't play with you anymore if…I won't help you anymore if…

Have you altered your relationships and now wonder why things are different? Try to keep in mind that for every action…there is a reaction. Have you changed your "sign off" with some members of your family or friends? How have other things changed and why? Have you spoken "about" the person instead of "to" the person? Simple questions but...they are not so easy to answer. It is very difficult to take responsibility for our part in unsmooth relationships.

It's easy to love someone when we agree. To love "**un**conditionally" is to love others like God loves us. The true test comes when we don't agree and there are no ifs, ands, or buts about it. This is "**un**conditional love" and it makes a whole world of difference in how we treat others.

"To love is a beautiful, mysterious event; do not miss it. Be neither too cautious nor too absorbed. Too many of us reason with our hearts and experience with our heads. It cannot be so. The heart knows no logic beyond need and desire; the head has no senses except the common and the pragmatic. Neither, frankly, is useful in love anyway. Rely on your sixth sense, that little voice within. There is no preparation for or protection from the joy and pain of relationships. They are inseparable twins. One follows another. And make no mistake, love is not gay abandon; it is to be courageous, to take risks and be disciplined." ~ Ramya Varma

3 ~ The Big Copout

No expectations...no disappointment...no resentment. Not too long ago, I had an interesting conversation with one of my adult daughters. She was actually quizzing me about child rearing practices and expectations. On this particular day, she wasn't pleased with the behavior of one of her children. She mentioned that when she and her sisters were growing up, that they just knew that their father and I had expectations of them. She went on to say that she innately knew by those expectations just how far she could go. For instance, she understood that she was expected to get good grades in school, to behave in an acceptable manner whether we were there to witness it or not, to get a higher education and to excel in her efforts to be all that she could be no matter her walk in life. This daughter also told me that our having expectations of her and her sisters helped set the bar for their personal growth and success because they learned to have reasonable goals and expectations of themselves.

My husband and I have always had expectations of ourselves. We are both goal oriented and have set numerous personal and couple targets over the years. We then worked hard to attain these sometimes difficult goals, which at times, stretched not only over the span of weeks or months, but over several years. When we failed, and we did fail on more than one occasion, we just tried harder and prayed for the guidance that we needed in order to succeed. Although, the success may not have come in the form we necessarily expected, it did indeed come. This concept taught us patience, trust, and enhanced our faith to know that there was a Divine guidance in our lives that would reward our efforts in an unexpected and refreshing way. However, nonetheless, we were not disappointed in the results of those expectations regardless the outcome.

When I look at the world around me, I think it is a positive attribute to have reasonable expectations of others, especially if I have expectations of myself and my loved ones. Although, in my opinion, it is necessary to differentiate between having reasonable expectations of others and "**un**conditional love". When and if, people don't live up to our expectations, our love should not be withdrawn. We love them no matter what the circumstance. When I have expectations of others, I am actually showing that love by treating them as a peer. In fact, I am complimenting my husband, children, family, friends and maybe even the stranger on the street. I am demonstrating my love and high regard for them because I see these individuals in the same light as I see myself. To me, to not have any expectations of others is to infer that they are less than me. I do not look at my friends or others in this way.

I consider this type of behavior…having no expectations…as a method of behavior utilized to avoid disappointment. In doing so, I am setting the bar so low that the people in my life can't help but look like winners. I liken it to letting others win at a game on purpose. However, the stakes are much higher now because this is the game of life and it's a far cry from child's play. I've been there and this kind of imbalance in a relationship is not very rewarding for either party. It inevitably results in a no win situation. To expect nothing may appear admirable at first blush but under further scrutiny and analysis, it is more of a copout than anything else. Those who prefer to or choose to merely give in a relationship and never receive, is not what I would even classify as a relationship in the first place. This type of situation will only evolve into a resentful and unrewarding pseudo-relationship in the long run.

To opt for this kind of unfulfilling encounter, not only implies that I am capable of giving more to others, the underlying action implies that others are less than me because they are unwilling or unable to give. It grants me, what I consider to be, the upper hand and suggests that the people in my life are needy and I am not. It does nothing for a person's self-esteem to even hint at the idea that they may have nothing to give back, even if it is as simple as a smile to a stranger on the street. When we expect nothing of others what are we really saying? Are we intimating that we don't need them or what they have to offer? Think about it. It is not always easy to admit that we have needs.

Relationships or friendships imply an affinity, kinship, or connection to other human beings. My friends are very much equal to me and I treat them as such and expect the same from them. It is unacceptable for me to be treated as less in any of my relationships. I expect my friends to be able to count on me during both the good times and the bad. I am no more chosen to just give to them than they are chosen to just give to me. We are all meant to give and receive on this earth. These kinds of reciprocal and respectful relationships are what make up the fabric of lasting and true friendships. This is why I have chosen to have reasonable expectations of my friends. They are as capable of giving as I am. We are the same. For that, I am eternally grateful because I very much need their prayers, their love, their support, and their encouragement just as much as I hope they need mine. I would like to think that our needs are mutually acceptable, albeit, they may occur at different times in our journey. I am truly honored when they embrace the fact that they can count on me and I want to be able to count on them too as I face both the joys and sorrows that life has to offer.

It is our mutual love and respect for each other, as well as the give and take in all healthy relationships, that have made them all the more precious to me. It has also given these kinships the strength they require to stand the test of time. It would be an ideal world if we could all be in a position to only give but I know full well that it has been a humbling experience for me to admit that I need to receive as well. This humbling experience has reminded me of the necessity for more humility in my life by accepting that I too, am needy, at times. How about you? Does it bring you comfort to know that you are not alone when it comes to facing trials and tribulations? Do you avoid having expectations of others to prevent yourself from being disappointed if they don't deliver? Do you see yourself as more giving in your relationships and then fall into the trap of resenting others when they don't reciprocate your generosity?

There is plenty to reflect upon when it comes to our family relationships and friendships. Please take a few moments to dwell on the answers to these questions and how they really affect you. Be honest now…remember it's just between you and your Maker.

"We all mold one another's dreams. We all hold each other's fragile hopes in our hands. We all touch others' hearts...." ~ Source Unknown.

"The sculptor will chip off all the unnecessary material to set free the angel. Nature will chip and pound us remorselessly to bring out our possibilities. She will strip us of wealth, humble our pride, humiliate our ambition, let us down from the ladder of fame, will discipline us in a thousand different ways if she can develop a little character....There is no medicine like hope, no incentive so great, and no tonic so powerful as expectation of something tomorrow." ~ Orison Swett Marden

4 ~ You Are Not Broken ~
Andrea Ayotte Cockerill

Although the memory of our first breath when we entered this world is beyond our recollection, its innocence and wonder are no less profound. You just have to look at your own or any newborn child to see the vulnerability and utter newness of when a new soul begins its journey into the experience of being a human being. When babies grow into toddlers, you can see the fearlessness of children's innate curiosity and how it propels them into following any and all of their hearts desires, which on many occasions goes against that of their mothers!

Imagine living this way as an adult, following your heart's desires with wild abandon. At some point in our childhood we go from living fearlessly, to viewing the world as unsafe. We start to realize that not all is right with the world and we may eventually internalize it as meaning that all is not right with us. At a deep level we turn from the experience of the newborn, a being of pure perfection, to feeling as if we are someone who is broken and in need of fixing. How painful it is to see ourselves in this light. We then start the process of seeing ourselves as possessing much darker traits.

Many people may not even realize that they actually think this way because it goes beyond the awareness stage. It is at a subconscious level as evidenced by the words we say to ourselves about our lives. How many times have we said, if such and such happens, then I will feel good, be happy, find joy, be worthy of love, etc.? This kind of thinking implies that at the core of our being, something is broken. We then project this brokenness onto the surface areas of our lives, our job, our bodies, our families, our communities and the list goes on. Isn't it easier to try to fix that, which is outer, than to go deep within ourselves and feel the emotion of brokenness, vulnerability and just plain not measuring up?

In my opinion, we spend so much time protecting ourselves and our spirit, trying to fix that which is truly not broken. Yes…you are not broken. There is nothing to fix. The center of your being is pure perfection and light. It is the part of you that always was and always will be. You can't lose it, damage it, abandon it, or escape the love that resides in you. You may have developed coping mechanisms along the way to protect yourself which have created layers similar to that of an onion. With compassion and faith, each of these layers can be carefully peeled away to reveal the wonder and innocence you came with when you entered into this world as pure perfection itself.

When you learn to view yourself as whole, failure won't have such a high price tag. It won't run so deep and healing won't take so long after you stumble and fall. Highs and lows would be just a part of life because the thread running through life's challenges would originate from a feeling of innate wholeness and love. I pray for this for myself, for all women and for all humankind. I pray each one of us experiences the joy of living with wild abandon like that of an innocent child.

When I was young, I was innocent and saw the world as limitless. Now that I am older, I may see the limits of this world, but my faith sees the limitlessness of God. It is this faith that allows me to spread my wings and take a chance on life. Are you willing to take that chance too….to look deep within yourself and find that childlike love and innocence that you were born with?

"We are all born for love. It is the principle of existence, and its only end." ~ *Benjamin Disraeli*

"Love is the emblem of eternity: it confounds all notions of time: effaces all memories of a beginning, all fear of an end." ~ *Anna Louise De Stael*

5 ~ He's Got the Whole World in His Hands

I am the mother of three married daughters. I have eight delightful grandchildren and still hope to be blessed with even more. I always knew that I loved my children with all my heart but I had no way of knowing until I became a grandmother that I would love my grandchildren with the same depth. Each time a grandchild is born, I feel the same thrill as when I gave birth to their mothers.

When we raise a family we all go through the trials and tribulations that come with each phase of growing up. I remember thinking to myself that after all three daughters were married and settled down, I would have a lot less to worry about and more time to merely sit back and enjoy the fun stuff. I must admit that this was one naive thought.

As my family continues to multiply I find that I actually have more to worry about, not less. Now my daughters are experiencing some of the woes of raising their children and I am well aware of almost everything that they are going through. I try my best to encourage them to "not sweat" the small stuff. I must admit though that it's not always easy to follow my own advice. One of the things I still "sweat" about is childhood illnesses especially in the younger grandchildren. The older ones can at least tell you what's wrong when they're not feeling good but the little ones can only cry about it. Is it only in my own mind or has there been an increase in childhood illnesses? When these little ones get sick, I'm so concerned in a way that brings out the worrywart in me.

It is at these times that I have to search inside and draw from the same strength I used when my daughters were young. That strength is my faith. I know that each and every child born on earth is a whole world to God. I also know that He's got the whole world in His hands. Of that, I am sure. I not only desire to trust in Him, I very much *need* to trust in Him for the benefit of all just like my daughters *need* to do so as well.

Yes indeed…it is wonderful to have been blessed with such an ever-growing family and I thank God on a daily basis. Nevertheless, I re-iterate, it is not only the family that is multiplying but also the fears and concerns that go with it. I need my faith now more than ever in order to encourage my daughters. I want to be there for them as much as possible as they face what life has to offer. I heard many years ago, that you never fully realize how much you believe in God until you have children. I couldn't agree more! We need prayers and our faith as we work through the challenges that go with raising a family. Don't you agree? What do you do when you are faced with family crises? Who do you turn to? How has your faith helped you cope with the challenges of raising a family?

"Worrying is carrying tomorrow's load with today's strength----carrying two days at once. It is moving into tomorrow ahead of time. Worrying doesn't empty tomorrow of sorrows, it empties today of strength." ~ *Corrie Ten Boom*

"There are many truths of which the full meaning cannot be realized until personal experience has brought it home." ~ *John Stuart Mill*

6 ~ The Jongleur

I have French heritage. My dad's first language was French and I married a Frenchman just like him. Now, over forty years later when I look at my husband, I can hardly believe how much he resembles my dad. Perhaps, it is only in his mannerisms but I see more. He not only looks like him if that is possible…it is how he acts…what he says and…also how he says it. I have always loved my French background, but I have never fulfilled my dream of carrying on a conversation in the French language that I love so much.

Many years ago when I was experiencing bouts of serious depression, I used to have long periods of silence. I spent a lot of hours thinking about what was happening to me…thinking about how I had arrived at this point…and thinking about what I was going to do to positively change my lot in life. One of the French words for "to think" is "jongler". When I had some of these episodes of deep thought, my husband frequently queried me about what was going on in my mind. It was more out of concern for me than anything else. He wanted to know what I was so deeply dwelling upon in order to better help me deal with these troubling thoughts.

He knew how much I loved the French language and oftentimes he would insert French words into our English conversations. He would therefore ask me what I was "jongling" about on a regular basis. His goal was to please me as well as to bring me out of that moment of despair and into our present day state of affairs. He could tell by the expression on my face that I was troubled as I was mulling over things in my mind in order to make more sense of them.

Now, almost thirty years later, I am writing about these very thoughts in an open and forthright way. In many instances, I use the voice of the "jongleur" to do so. For those of you who don't know, the "jongleur" is a French minstrel who used to make his way from town to town to entertain people in the olden days. At times, he utilized stories or music to help do this. When I write, it is done in much the same fashion. I usually incorporate much humor…many quotes… anecdotes…and personal stories to entertain my readers. I do this to make a variety of points as well as a method of sharing my personal philosophy on life.

Now that I have succeeded in sorting through my puzzling thoughts, I feel much more comfortable, not only in sharing them with my husband and my family but with others as well. I consider myself to be a present day jongleur as I share my written musings with you. I sincerely hope that you find pleasure in getting to know me better and that you derive some benefit from my writing and what I have to say. The point to my inspirational writing is not about wanting to say something; it's more about my actual *need* to say it. Do you feel the *need* to say something that is going on in your life? Are you being an effective communicator and getting the meaning of your words and feelings across to those who care about you? In order to establish deeper and more intimate relationships, we must endeavor to become more proficient communicators. Once again, I ask. Are you readily and honestly getting your messages across to those you love and care for? Are you being true to yourself?

"We must become acquainted with our emotional household; we must see our feelings as they actually are. This breaks their hypnotic and damaging hold on us." ~ *Vernon Howard*

7 ~ The Three R's

For those of you who have read my background information in the Introduction, you already know that I am a former elementary school teacher. During my teaching years, I spent a great deal of time teaching the three R's of education; that of, *r*eading, *r*iting and *r*ithmetic as they were so fondly called in those days.

Today we are utilizing many other words that start with the letter R such as recycle, reuse, and restore in an effort to be energy conscious and to help protect and sustain our environment.

Although, I left the classroom many years ago, the classroom has never left me. Once a teacher, always a teacher! It's in my blood. In fact, my other published books are what I consider to be teaching tools. My words are never meant to offend but rather, to educate. The reason I have chosen to discuss the three R's of education is pretty straightforward. Other than the ones I have already mentioned in the first two paragraphs, there are many more equally important words starting with the letter R.

A few of these are responsibility, respect, and reciprocity/relationship building. When people hold themselves accountable for their actions, they demonstrate a sense of responsibility. Consequently, when they become more accountable and accept responsibility, these individuals develop self-respect and in turn earn the respect of others. By earning the respect of others, this concept eventually results in a mutually respectful relationship. This is what I refer to as the beginnings of a reciprocal connection or affinity. Simply put, what goes around comes around.

As I whisper now to you...whether positive or negative, people eventually become the reflection of each other. In other words, those around you will be a reflection of yourself and your values. How is your reflection in the mirror looking back at you? Do you like what you see? Usually the people around us are the most similar to us because like-minded individuals have the tendency to gravitate toward each other. Do you like and enjoy those around you? If not, why? If so, you might very well ask yourself the same thing in order to get a better picture of who you are and what you're all about. I re-iterate...do you like what you see? Trust me this is a very important question but not nearly as important as your answer.

"As human beings we are endowed with freedom of choice, and we can not shuffle off our responsibility upon

the shoulders of God or nature. We must shoulder it ourselves. It is up to us." ~ Arnold J. Toynbee

8 ~ Confidence in God

Have you ever been given a precious gift with very little monetary value that means so much to you? Many years ago, long before my father passed away, he gave each of his children a booklet titled "Confidence in God ~ Words of Encouragement" by Rev. Daniel Considine S. J. It is very small, about 3" by 5"...and has 94 pages. What I didn't realize at the time was quite how dear this little gift meant to me. I thoroughly enjoyed reading it and have done so on numerous occasions since. Unfortunately, I no longer have the original booklet. I merely have a copy that I purchased at a later date. What actually made the first one so very special to me was my father's signature inside...to my daughter Dolores...love Dad.

Upon receiving this token of love, I was so thrilled with its content that I shared this booklet with the mother of one of the students I was teaching at the time. I wanted to pass along its beautiful message. I soon regretted my decision but it was too late to do anything about it. I now wish I had kept that original little gift from my father and just given away one of the new booklets that I purchased at a later date but it was after the fact. The original booklet soon became so priceless to me, yet I had parted with it without a moment's thought or the slightest hesitation. I eventually purchased several more of these very booklets and gave them away as delightful little gifts myself.

The content remains the same and although the message in it is very dear to me and still holds true today, my replacement booklet does not have that personal inscription from my father. I miss him and the special touch of his loving words that have come to mean so much to me over the years. Today I am much more sentimental. Years ago, in my haste and with the right intentions, I gave away a gift that cannot be replaced. Every time I read my copy of "Confidence in God" I think of my Dad and I long to see his signature inside. Have you ever done that? Have you ever given away some priceless, little gift that cannot be replaced no matter how hard you try?

I want to share a quote with you from this booklet. When I randomly opened the pages, this was the first one to jump out at me. *"It is no small penance in these days merely to bear with yourself; and if you bear properly with yourself and your neighbor, God will give you the highest graces."* I would have to say that this is the message that God would like us to hear today.

Yes…merely to bear properly with yourself and your neighbor. So much easier said than done, don't you think?

Please think about this today as you make your way on whatever path lays ahead for you. Just for today…tomorrow will come soon enough.

"God does not require you to follow His leading on blind trust. Behold the evidence of an invisible intelligence pervading everything, even your own mind and body." ~ *Raymond Holliwell*

9 ~ First Things First

"From our childhood many of us have been told more of the punishments God has in store for us if we fail to please Him than the rewards He looks forward to giving when we do please Him....The first thing in loving our Lord is to believe Him lovable. What are the sorts of persons one loves? First, they must be easy to get on with. How many in their heart of hearts think our Lord easy to get on with? We think Him touchy, unapproachable, easily annoyed or offended. And yet all this fear of Him pains Him very much. Would our father wish us to hang our heads, be shy and shrinking in his presence? How much less so our Heavenly Father? He has an almost foolish love for us." **(Rev. Daniel Considine in "Confidence in God~Words of Encouragement")**

How many of you can relate to this quote? How many of you can think back to your childhood and remember the fear that was instilled in you? How many of you remember hearing about the fires of eternal damnation and that you would burn there if you didn't do what God wanted? Yes...we learned full well the punishments of God!

On the other hand, how many of you, in your early childhood, ever heard that God loved you? I, for one, didn't.

In all the teachings I learned as a child, I never once recall hearing the word *Love* to describe how God felt about me or anyone else for that matter. If you are in my age bracket, the word God and *Love* never went hand in hand. The word reward was never heard either. The word punishment definitely was used to describe what God was all about and what His plans for us would be if we didn't toe the line. How much damage was done to some of the children of my era? Are you one of them?

I think Rev. Daniel Considine has it right. It took me twenty-five years to write *I'm Not Perfect & It's Okay*. It's hard to believe it took me that long to put pen to paper and write my first book. In actuality, it took me that long to garner the courage and determination to set the record straight. God loves me, warts and all and He loves you too!

Take a moment to reflect on all the little ways God shows His *Love* for you. At times, we are so busy with are lives that we miss what is "hiding in plain sight". Yes…please just take a moment to be grateful for your life.

"The cure for all the ills and wrongs, the cares, the sorrows, and the crimes of humanity, all lie in that one word 'love'. It is the divine vitality that everywhere produces and restores life." ~ Lydia Maria Child

10 ~ Psst...Hey EWE!

Yes you! Now that I've caught your attention I really want to talk to you. By chance, do you enjoy doing Crosswords and other types of puzzles? If so, this is the chapter for you.

Ever since I can remember, I have been a puzzle solver. I truly love the mental challenge of trying to figure things out. It is unbelievable how mentally stimulating and life enriching these puzzles can be. In most local newspapers, there is a wealth of knowledge at our fingertips just ready to be tapped into on a daily basis.

Now why did I choose the word EWE in my title to get your attention? Most of you probably know that EWE is another word for a female sheep. Over and over again this word comes up in Crossword Puzzles. Every time I see it when solving a puzzle, it reminds me of Jesus Christ and how He is described as the gentle Lamb. If we are to emulate Christ and follow in His footsteps we, too, must be like gentle lambs in our dealings with people.

As we all know, it is not always easy to be gentle and kind. Many times in life, our patience is tested as we become frustrated with the people around us. In some instances, people may be unaware of this fact but on other occasions we may only be fooling ourselves into thinking that they don't take notice of exactly how we feel. The tone of our voice and our body language can quickly give away our true feelings despite what our words may say.

I find as I do my daily Crossword Puzzle that God works in mysterious ways. I hear God's Word many times as I solve these puzzles. I can do an examination of conscience and ask myself if I have had any cross…words with any one in my life. God can prompt me on several occasions throughout these puzzles if I am open to His cues/clues. He reminds me to emulate the gentle Lamb that so aptly demonstrates a mother's love. In doing so, it gives me the desire to follow in His footsteps when I come across the word EWE.

Other times, one of the clues will ask for the letters found on the cross. Yes…INRI. Again, I am reminded that the Lamb died on the cross for the salvation of humankind. This inscription reinforces the fact that I have sinned and Jesus' forgiveness is so great that He chose to die on the cross to save my soul and yours too. He is the Teacher and I am the student. Frequently, I need to be reminded to be ready to forgive at all times because my transgressions have so generously been forgiven.

It is truly amazing to see the many creative ways that God can reach out to people. God has a way of utilizing all of

His followers and reminding them of their mission in life. We only need to be open to hearing the message whenever and wherever it presents itself.

God is very creative indeed. He knows our regular haunts and just when and how to reach us in order to get His worthwhile message across. I much prefer Crosswords to cross...words, if EWE know what I mean. How about you? Have you said some angry words lately that you aren't feeling too good about...or has someone offended you by their harsh words? As challenging and enjoyable as solving Crossword puzzles may be, we all know that it is far harder to solve the dilemmas created by our cross words with others. Yes...we have all been there whether on the giving end or the receiving end. Most often, we struggle with solving this type of problem and could use a Higher Power to guide us. Wouldn't you agree?

"The very greatest things...great thoughts, discoveries, inventions...have usually been nurtured in hardship, often pondered over in sorrow, and at length established with difficulty." ~ Samuel Smiles

11 ~ The Absence Of

I know...you're never supposed to end a sentence with a preposition, but perhaps I can make an exception in this case because I have merely ended a title with one. I find that when I write, I take a few creative liberties and bend some of the grammatical rules as I see fit. Some fellow authors may very well choose to do the same. I hope so because as liberal minded as I may think I am, it always feels good to know that I am not totally alone with any particular point of view.

Today, I am about to express one of those views. The other day, I read a neat email sent to me by a long time Christian friend. This article really got me thinking about some of my own "isms". The theme of the article had to do with opinions on science versus the existence of God. I'm not going to go on and on about what I read because I want to zero in on what captured my attention the most.

First of all, it was the concept of the description of death as the "absence of life". The article mentioned that you cannot scientifically measure death so therefore, death should be referred to as the "absence of life". This concept is quite clear and easily understood. As I continued to read, it was obvious to me that this article was fast becoming more philosophical than scientific because God was described as the Light, while evil was described as the "absence of Light". In other words, those of us without God in our lives would be living in darkness. I'm pretty sure we have all heard this phrase before to describe different aspects of Christian faith or lack of it.

As a result of some introspection, this concept made me look at my faith from another angle. It reminded me of the story about Jesus fishing in the stormy waters with His disciples. When they kept their eyes on Him, the apostles had faith and knew no fear. They were unafraid of the dark skies and the turbulent waters surrounding them and the imminent risk they posed. However, the exact opposite happened when they lost their focus and stopped looking at Jesus. Perhaps, the same theory holds true for us. The "absence of faith" results in fear. When we are afraid, when we feel fear…is it because we really have something to fear or is it because we have taken our eyes off of Jesus? Do we give the concept of fear "life" and let it have power over us and what we choose to do or not do?

It is very difficult to overcome fear. I try my best to remember what Jesus taught us about perfect love casting out fear. Jesus offers His perfect, unconditional love. I do not want to be afraid. I want to know, love and serve the Lord with a deep abiding faith with the "absence of fear". When I feel fear, it seems that I have done the exact opposite. I have taken my eyes off of Jesus and I experience the "absence of faith". I much prefer to have it the other way around. I also need to remind myself that the word "fear" can mean "to be in awe" or "to have reverence and respect" in some instances.

My relationship with God is one of those instances. I have every desire to be in "awe" of the God who created me out of love rather than to be afraid of making mistakes and fearing His retribution for my human weaknesses.

I do not want to live with the impression that I am constantly being judged by my Creator who is ready to punish me if I take a wrong turn. For in reality, He wants to show me nothing but His infinite love and mercy, not only for me, but for all His creatures. I once "feared" God but in all honestly is was the wrong kind of "fear". I "feared" punishment and retribution rather than being in "awe" of the loving Father that I now readily embrace. How do you view God? Are you afraid? Do you act out of true love and a desire to please our Maker or do you do the right thing for the wrong reason. "Fear" of being punished? I gently ask you to think about it…really think about it. Your answer may very well surprise you. There is such a fine line to walk and it's very easy to mix up the two emotions.

"Most of our obstacles would melt away if, instead of cowering before them, we should make up our minds to walk boldly through them." ~ Orison Swett Marden

12 ~ Love Triangle ~ Fred Ayotte

I know many of you have heard of a love triangle where two people love the same person. In this situation, the two suitors usually don't like each other at all. This happened to me during my thirties and forties with my wonderful wife.

In my late thirties, on the thirteenth birthday of one of my twin daughters, she acquired a brownish-red, miniature poodle named Joey. He was a very beautiful dog. However, as time went by in our house, Joey came to believe that he and my wife were the married couple and that I was the odd man out.

Many times I had to set him straight. For instance, my wife always went to bed a few hours earlier than me. At that time, Joey would jump onto the bed and sleep on my side of the bed. When I retired later, he did not want to move. I had to physically remove him (very gently) and put him on the floor so that I could get into my side of the bed. There were many other similar events like this where he thought I was the third wheel in our house and I had to set him straight yet again. Needless to say, I was not a big fan of his and he wanted very little to do with me on several occasions.

Many years later, when my daughter eventually got her own place, she took Joey with her. Well, as you know, dogs do not have as long a life span as humans. In his thirteenth year, Joey became quite sick. After numerous trips to the vet, we knew it was just a matter of time until he would have to be put down in order to prevent him from needless suffering.

A few days before he passed away, we just so happened to be visiting at our daughter's apartment. I was sitting on a chair when Joey came right up to me and just sat on his haunches right at my feet. I automatically reached down to pick him up and he didn't put up a fuss like he normally did. He just sat on my lap very quietly without even trying to move or get down.

A few days later he passed away. I know, even if no one else believes me that Joey came to me before he died so we could make amends for our relationship. In his own way he was forgiving me for my behavior or asking me to forgive him. I will never know for sure but either way was fine with me. It's too bad, we as humans; oftentimes, can't or won't be anywhere near as forgiving as Joey. What a wonderful world this would be if we were. What do you think? Is there something to be learned from our animal friends? Do you need to reach out and forgive someone or perhaps you are in need of forgiveness today?

"Friendship is the only cement that will ever hold the world together." ~ Woodrow Wilson

13 ~ Positive Attitude

I recall going bowling a few times in my younger years. To be honest, I do not have an athletic bone in my body. This one time, I got the worst score possible. It was so embarrassing! The bowling alley was full of fun-loving people and I didn't even realize that anyone had been watching me until after the game. This older gentleman came up to me and introduced himself as a minister.

He said something which has stuck in my mind all these years... something that I didn't even realize I was doing because it came so naturally to me. Obviously he could see how badly I was bowling. It was pretty apparent to everyone in or around the vicinity. He proceeded to tell me that after every ball I threw, no matter how bad it was, I would turn around and smile at my fellow bowlers. He then told me how wonderful he thought this was. *Wow...it was like, how could anyone smile after bowling the way that I did!* I was so grateful for the compliment that I thanked him and then gave him one of my biggest smiles. It meant the world to me that someone had given me such a fine a compliment. That's me in a nutshell, forever the smiley one...forever the eternal optimist. You know the one...the one, who would be searching for a dog if she found a pile of dung in the garage while someone else would be cursing the mess. I would think that someone probably gave me a new puppy as a gift and I would be busy trying to find it. There could be no other explanation! Right?

You want to know my secret? I can usually find the bright side to just about anything. This has been my saving grace in facing the many ups and downs of daily living. It has been said that *"it is worth a thousand dollars a year to have the habit of looking on the bright side of things"*. ~ *Orville Gilbert Brim* So in other words, it is probably where some of my greatest wealth lies because in most instances this is exactly how I choose to view life. Choose is the key word here. In life we have many choices and our attitude usually has a huge impact on how we view life. I guess you could always ask yourself if you see your *"glass as half empty or half full"*. Your answer might give you a better understanding of what I mean. Do you consider yourself to have a positive attitude? If so, is this actually the image you are portraying?

I have a little line I use with my husband now and then. When someone tells me they are happy but I just can't tell by their expression, I say that perhaps, "they should tell their face". Do you have a down-at-the-mouth expression, lifeless eyes, or a chip on your shoulder? If you do, I can guarantee that your face shows it. Check it out and see for yourself. Take a moment to smile in the mirror and see if your eyes light up with joy. Do they? Do you want an instant, cost free face lift...if so, all you need to do is smile as often as possible. I guarantee you that it will take years off your face. I have observed this phenomenon for a very long time. Perhaps, you should just start there. See for yourself by observing the smiles on the faces of those around you. I certainly wish you could tell me the results of this little experiment...but then, what matters most is that you take me at my word and check it out for yourself.

"The greatest discovery of my generation is that human beings can alter their lives by altering their attitudes of mind." ~ William James

"The greatest power that a person possesses is the power to choose" ~ J. Martin Kohe

14 ~ The Truth

The truth..."*It may not lead you to where you thought you were going, but it will always lead you somewhere better. When ignored, it will eventually show itself. The closeness of your relationships is directly proportional to the degree to which you have revealed the truth about yourself. It can be painful*". ~ Source Unknown

It is not always easy to have honest and open relationships. The more honest the relationship, the more vulnerable we become...it is one of the reasons that we choose to wear masks in life. We do this to protect ourselves from what others may think or say about us. We usually try to put our best foot forward in order to impress people. The more comfortable we become in a relationship, the more we feel safe to take down these barriers.

The truth... "*It's a process of peeling away the layers of your false self, your trying-to-be-something-you're-not self, your copycat self, your trying-to-sound-a-certain-way self, your spent-my-life-watching-television self. It's like going to psychotherapy, delving deep and allowing the real* *you to emerge; only in this case you want it to find its way on to the page." ~ Rachelle Gardner*

Yes, the truth may not lead you to where you thought you were going but would you want it any other way?

The truth…if and when you choose to embrace it, has a way of cleansing your soul like a pleasant rain that falls ever so gently and washes away all your weaknesses.

The truth…gives us the courage to face all that life offers.

The truth…if you are an author, is why we have chosen to write and to bare our souls to those who honor us by reading our words. Yes, the truth for those who seek it, can find its way to the page. May you feel the mist on your face that mingles with your tears as you wash away your woes when you…humbly and sincerely…discover the truth in your life. I don't mean **your** truth…I mean **the** truth. There is a definite and distinctive difference in the way we perceive things and the way that they actually are.

Please take a moment to reflect on this truism. Do you know the truth about your life, your actions, the motive behind those actions and what it means to have the strength and courage to face the reality of your choices? Merely respond with the plain truth and no prettying up of the facts. In all honesty, it is never easy to really face the facts and the part we may have played in any given situation.

"Reality isn't the way you wish things to be, nor the way they appear to be, but the way they actually are." ~ *Robert J. Ringer*

15 ~ On Being Judgmental

Once again, I had an interesting conversation with one of my daughters a short time ago. In this conversation, she used the word 'judgmental' as a negative or undesirable trait. She mentioned during this conversation that she did not want to be a 'judgmental' person. I have also heard other people say such statements as "I'm tired of being judged". I find the use of this word rather foreign to me. I personally, seldom if ever, feel like I am being judged by others. Perhaps, some people do judge me and I just don't recognize it. Therefore, I can't honestly say for sure whether I have been judged in the past or not. However, as an author, I find that it is necessary for me to have a wide variety of opinions. It would be pretty difficult to write books, articles, or blogs without having them.

I know that I am not the only one with observational skills and personal opinions. I also know that it is required in all walks of life in order to be able to accurately assess situations and people. Oftentimes this habit results in making more informed decisions. As the years go by, I find that I am better able to analyze what I am observing and where these observations will lead me. It would seem that this skill is enhanced by a combination of age plus experience. At this time, in order to better make my point, I am going to get a little philosophical and use an analogy to better explain my assessment of the use of the word 'judgmental'.

Many years ago when I suffered from depression, which is considered to be a form of mental illness, I was ashamed about my condition and chose to hide this fact from my family and friends as much as possible. I felt that there was a "stigma" attached to mental illness and I did not want anyone to know. Therefore, I kept it a well-hidden secret except from my husband and my parents. Even so, they never knew the full extent of my suffering or despair. I managed to hide it from them to varying degrees as well. Now, after almost thirty years, I am able to not only write about my experiences but if the appropriate opportunity arises, I am far more willing to discuss what I went through.

The conclusion I arrived at after all these years, is that I actually had a bias myself. I know it was a learned bias based on my personal frame of reference, but it was a bias nonetheless. At the time of my illness, I was projecting how I thought society in general, viewed mental illness when I was the one actually thinking it. Does that make sense? If I didn't have my own bias toward mental illness, I would have been far more open and forthright about it in the first place regardless of what anyone thought. Are you still with me here?

Okay, now I want to return to the concept of 'being judgmental' or the feeling of 'being judged'. I think the same rationale I used for admitting to my own prejudice also applies here. Perhaps, people who sense that they are being judged have that trait in their own personality. If they think they are being judged in any way, shape, or form, maybe it is because they are actually judgmental towards others themselves. If a trait is part of our own character make up, we might assume that others share this same trait as well. Does this make sense to you?

We can and do project the emotions that we are dealing with on others. We actually have no idea what other people are thinking. If we choose to express our views on other people's thoughts, we are only sharing what is going on in our own minds and assuming that they think the same way. What I'm basically trying to say is this. What we think we see in others may actually live within ourselves. The only way we can ever really know what someone else is thinking is if or when they decide to share their thoughts with us. Also, it is a well-known adage that the very things we don't like about others are what we actually don't like about ourselves. Is this ideology familiar to you? If so, perhaps, it's time to have a better look about *why* we dislike certain individuals and *what* we can do about it. A better understanding of ourselves often leads to a better understanding and acceptance of those around us.

"We are only falsehood, duplicity, contradiction; we both conceal and disguise ourselves from ourselves." ~ Blaise Pascal

"A clear understanding of negative emotions dismisses them." ~ Vernon Howard

16 ~ Connecting the Dots

When you were a young child, did you ever have the opportunity to do "connect the dot" pictures in your activity/coloring book? I know they still have these enjoyable little learning tools today as I've seen my children and now my grandchildren receive the same pleasure that I did as a young child when engaging in this type of fun. After joining the numbers or connecting the dots, they too, can see the picture and then color it in.

In life, I envision God's Plan as much the same. From my point of view, it's similar to a bunch of dots which are in the processing of being connected so that His Divine Plan or picture will eventually be revealed to us as humankind. Over the last several weeks and months, I have touched base with many fellow authors and have had the opportunity to feel very connected to these gifted people. One referred to this experience as a "God thing"...another referred to it as a "God connection". As to be expected, it feels wonderful to connect with other like-minded individuals in the atmosphere of love, acceptance, and co-operation. I personally refer to it as connecting the dots, with the dots actually being the people in our lives. This opportunity helps to further unveil what God has in store for us as we work together toward achieving a common goal. When these moments occur, I can tell you that it feels so right, just like when we were children and we finished our "dot-to-dot" picture. Although just like when we were young, we might occasionally connect the wrong dots in the picture. As adults, we may also connect the wrong dot in our dealings with people. At these times, it usually doesn't look or feel right. There's kind of a niggling inside of us that just won't leave us alone. At that point, we have to make a mental decision to retrace our steps and erase where we erred in order to get back on track. Does this ever happen to you? Are there some people in your life that you are not comfortable with and that you know you shouldn't have a relationship with them…or a least not at the present time?

At times, we can connect with a person whom at first blush appears to be a "dot" or a "God connection". After a while though, their behavior may change. Instead of working together for the common good, our relationship takes a negative turn. We might become unexpected competitors resulting in feelings of disappointment and resentment. These "friends" may start putting us down or taking what they require from us in order to succeed or further their own agenda. In the great scheme of things, if and when, we are striving to do God's Will here on earth, we are not competitors vying for some golden cup. The key is to help, support, and encourage each other because the prize is the same for us all.

When we don't positively or productively connect with people, we are not working toward the completion of God's Big Picture. This, in reality is supposed to be the common goal. We need each other. Are you a "dot" working toward the common goal or do you have your own personal agenda? What about those closest to you? Do you have your eyes on the same end result or are you wasting a lot of time and energy working against each other? Negative energy can be non-productive, very exhausting, and a total waste of precious time. I think the following quote sums it up pretty well.

"What I do you cannot do; but what you do, I cannot do. The needs are great, and none of us, including me, ever do great things. But we can all do small things, with great love, and together we can do something wonderful." ~ **Cindie Thomas**

17 ~ Child's Play...or is it?

I want to tell you a cute little story with a very big lesson in it. When I was a very young girl about six years old or so, I spent a great deal of time playing with the neighborhood kids. In those days, you could go freely from one house to the next without a lot of concern by your parents. One day a little girl named Yvette, asked me to come over and play dolls at her house. She was a bit younger than me but I was happy to play with her just the same. Right at the onset, she told me that she had already called on two other little girls (sisters) but they were having their afternoon nap. They actually did that in those days too, right up until you started school.

Yvette and I played for a least an hour in her back porch with her mother periodically checking up on us. We both had a wonderful time. Shortly thereafter, there was a knock on the door and there appeared the two sisters that Yvette originally wanted to play with. In they came and with that...out I went. Yvette promptly told me that I had to go home because now they could play with her and that was her original plan. As I mentioned earlier, she told me right up front that she had called on them first. I never gave it a moment's thought and I just got up and quietly left.

Within what felt like only a few minutes, Yvette came running down the sidewalk and asked me to come back and play. She explained to me that her mother came out to check on us and she discovered that I wasn't there anymore. From what I could gather, her mother asked where I was and Yvette admitted to her that she had sent me home. Her mother went on to say that it wasn't a kind thing to do. She then encouraged Yvette to go find me and invite me back to play dolls with her and the other two little girls. Her mother apparently saw no reason why the four of us couldn't just play together and neither did I. I quickly accepted her request and returned to Yvette's house. Her mother then treated us all to Popsicles.

I will never forget this incident as long as I live. Yvette is not the only one that learned a valuable lesson that day because I know something very much resonated with me. I don't know how many times I see adults treat their friends this exact same way except they are no longer at child's play. When someone else comes along, they might have the tendency to drop the friends they have and move on...or they have some kind of pecking list when it comes to the order of their friends. If their first choice is unavailable, they will simple go down their mental list in order to find someone who is free. Every time I see such unacceptable behavior I think of Yvette's mom. I wish she had been there for these people when they were young children so that they would know how to treat people in their adult life.

I've been told that we learn all we need to know as far as how we are supposed to treat others by the time we are in kindergarten. It doesn't hurt to remind ourselves of these little lessons so that we can treat our adult friends with the love and respect that they deserve. Good for Yvette's mom for taking the time to make a difference in her daughter's life, the lives of the other two little girls and mine as well. She will never fully know how much that act of kindness meant to me that memorable day so many years ago. Mothers have a very important job…in fact it may very well be the most instrumental and influential one in forming the values of our children. It is a wise thing to acknowledge this fact because mothers are the very first teachers in their children's lives. Do you remember any special childhood lessons? Do you still try to keep them in mind in your adult life? Treating people with love and respect never changes no matter what our age. Do unto others…yup, it's still applies today. Morals and values never go out of style.

"Only mothers can think of the future…because they give birth to it in their children." ~ Maxim Gorky

"There is no greater religion than human service. To work for the common good is the greatest creed." ~ Albert Schweitzer

"Life is a succession of lessons which must be lived to be understood." ~ Ralph Waldo Emerson

18 ~ Found Money

A strange thing happened to me on my morning walk. I usually walk two miles every morning with my husband but today he was off mowing our daughter's lawn. I decided to stick my ear plugs in and enjoy some music as I walked alone. I met a few people on my path. One was a jogger, another was a biker, and the final one was a mother with two young boys. As I walked along enjoying the music, I spotted a sealed envelope on the grassy boulevard that obviously all three of these people had missed. Initially, I thought someone had dropped a piece of mail so I picked it up and thought I would just pop it in the mail box for them. On closer inspection, I could see through the transparent window of the envelope that there was cash inside because I could see a $50 bill. On the front of it was written the name Gina ($200).

I have found money before but it is usually in the form of coins. I have also found the odd paper money but never have I found $200. About 30 years ago I found a $1 bill that has "Jesus Loves You" written on it and I still have it folded up in my wallet to this day. When I find this kind of money, it feels good. However, finding this $200 did not feel good at all. It reminded me of when my teenage daughter had a paper route. She was supposed to go shopping after school but when she used the rest room, she accidentally forgot her cash in an envelope by the sink. There was $100 in it and she was absolutely heartsick when she went to check at the lost and found and discovered that no one had turned it in. We helped her out by giving her some money but she has never forgotten that moment and neither have I.

Today when I found this cash, in my mind I saw the face of my heartsick daughter. Although I had no idea who Gina was or what she looked like, I knew in my heart I wanted to make an earnest effort to find her. I never opened the envelope nor did I put it in my pocket. I hoped someone would see me carrying it and claim it. I held the envelope in my hand visible for all to see just in case I passed by the owner of this cash. I kept my eyes open for someone who might be searching for it. As I backtracked, I ran into the woman with the young boys but now she was alone. She was going in the opposite direction with her back to me and I could see that she was on the phone. She didn't seem to be looking for a lost envelope but I decided to call out to her anyways...I yelled out "hi".

When she turned around, I asked if her name was Gina and she said "no". I was about to continue on my way when she called back to me. She then asked why I was looking for Gina because she knew her. She informed me that Gina was her children's babysitter. I explained that I had found an envelope with Gina's name on it. That's all, no more information than that. She then started to walk toward me. She looked so relieved as she told me that the envelope contained $200 and it fell out of the boys' lunch kit while they were walking to Gina's earlier in the morning. This is when I first encountered her. If you would have seen the look on this young mother's face. I think it was sheer disbelief bordering on shock when I handed her the sealed envelope with the $200 still in it. I may have made her day but you know something, she made mine too. It felt so rewarding to find her and give back what wasn't mine in the first place.

A very similar situation occurred a few years ago when my husband and I were at a very crowded flea market in Mesa, AZ. A young couple was walking ahead of us. The young man had his hands in his pockets and when he pulled one hand out, a big wad of money fell to the ground behind him. He was totally oblivious as my husband bent down to pick it up. My husband could have simply put it in his pocket or…we could have easily turned down an aisle or walked into a kiosk and went along our merry way. The couple just kept walking ahead of us until my husband tapped the fellow on the shoulder and said "You dropped your money". Seeing both their faces was priceless. They were totally speechless and obviously unbelievably grateful as shown by their shocked expressions. I know there's an old saying that goes like this "a fool and his money are soon parted" but in this case we were very willing to part with this found money. Neither my husband nor I are fools. It was not our money in either instance and we took great pleasure in returning it to the rightful owners. I wish someone had done that with my daughter all those years ago. Being honest gives us the opportunity to have more faith in humankind.

Take a moment to reflect upon some of your personal experiences or your own acts of kindness and how they made you feel...or reflect on a memory of an act of kindness bestowed upon you. Sometimes, the smallest act of kindness can have the most profound effect. Does it ever feel genuinely good to keep something that isn't rightfully yours? Is it not far more rewarding to exemplify the traits of honesty and integrity? To be sure, it is a fine example to set for others, especially our children and definitely a desirable behavior to emulate.

"You can never lose anything that really belongs to you, and you can't keep that which belongs to someone else." ~ Edgar Cayce

19 ~ Drip...Drop ~ A Christmas Thought

When we think about erosion in our environment, we may picture a huge wave beating against the wall of a cliff at sea. Eventually as it pounds away, the cliff caves in and the waves continue to erode the shore line.

In many of our personal relationships, the erosion that takes place doesn't always occur in the same dramatic way. Sometimes, it does take one big upset similar to a tsunami to end a relationship but usually it takes many years of neglect or even physical or emotional abuse. At times, our unacceptable or unattractive behavior is more subtle, like a lack of consideration or unkind behavior to those around us as the drip...drop of our uncaring ways eat away at the bond we may have once shared. The drip....drop may include gossip or maligning another person's reputation. The drip...drop may also include conditional love which is the act of forcing others to earn our love by their behavior.

Whether with family or friends, a continuous drip...drop of inappropriate behavior eventually takes its toll and the relationship caves in much like the major erosion previously described. To create and maintain a quality relationship, it is necessary to show that we care. We do this by taking the time to cultivate or maintain these special connections. In doing so, it is essential to put forth the much-needed effort in order to keep the relationship alive and healthy. In my opinion, if we don't do this, the relationship will not be very positive nor very rewarding. More than likely it will eventually die.

Caring about the people we love involves making them feel like a special part of our lives. It's not about taking them for granted but rather about showing our appreciation and love for them in some of the simplest ways...putting them first on the list instead of last, a special card, a visit...or any other small act of kindness that we may choose in order to let our family or friends know we love them.

Please, during this special Christmas Season as we celebrate the birth of Jesus, it is wise to remind ourselves to make room in the "Inn" of our hearts instead of allowing the drip...drop...of our behavior to force our family and friends into the stable of our lives. If that's where they are...perhaps we must ask ourselves why. Have we really and honestly made room at our "Inn" or have we made them feel like they belong outside? Having room at our "Inn" is a year-long activity not a once a year occasion.

Hopefully, the true meaning of Christmas and the celebration of Christ's birth will also be exemplified by our behavior between New Year's and Christmas, rather than the short week between Christmas and New Year's. In order to celebrate a wondrous, peaceful, and joyous Christ-filled Christmas, as well as an abundant year, it is necessary to make room in our "Inn" all year long! Is your Christmas Season one week long or do you celebrate the birth of Christ in your heart the other fifty-one weeks of the year?

"I am convinced that the world is not a mere bog in which men and women trample themselves in the mire and die. Something magnificent is taking place here amid the cruelties and tragedies, and the supreme challenge to intelligence is that of making the noblest and best in our curious heritage." ~ Charles A. Beard

20 ~ Christmas Love

The Christmas Season is upon us once again. It is only two short weeks until Christmas Eve. The hustle and bustle of Christmas is all around us as we hurry and scurry about to finish our shopping and plan for all the usual celebrations. I want to draw from some precious memories to stress the importance of keeping the true meaning of Christmas alive as we come to the end of another year. In order to do so, I am going to travel back into my own childhood and the memories that I cherish from so long ago.

When I was a young girl, Christmas was seldom about giving gifts. If I received one…it was usually an unwrapped and much-needed article. I considered myself blessed to receive any present at all. The excitement mounted in our home regardless of the lack of presents. Christmas Eve was the start of the family celebratory season with a midnight church service followed by the special treats of homemade "tortiere"/ meat pie and other Christmas delights.

My siblings and I would tie our stockings to our wrought iron bed and wait for morning with eager anticipation. Sometime during the night, my dad would creep into our bedroom and quietly put one Christmas orange, a few unshelled peanuts, and some hard unwrapped candy at the bottom of our long stockings...stockings that we actually wore and only used in this manner once a year for this special occasion. Even when we were very young, we never talked about Santa Claus. We seemed to always know that it was my Dad putting those few items in our stockings for which we were ever so grateful to receive.

To me, Christmas Love is really about family but even more importantly, it is about celebrating the birth of Christ. In doing so, we are sharing in the joy of the holy family of Jesus, Mary, and Joseph and that special birth of Our Savior that took place over 2000 years ago.

At times, it is apparent to me that society has taken the Christ out of Xmas and replaced it with many un-Christ-like substitutes...a multitude of X's. There is much Xtravagance, many unrealistic Xpectations, too much Xtra spending, Xaggerated gift giving, Xcessive eating, Xhaustion, and too many other Xmas activities to mention. In order to truly experience the meaning of Christmas Love, it is necessary to get back to basics and keep Christ in our Christmas festivities by removing as many X's as possible.

I also feel it is necessary to refocus and redefine what Christmas is all about and what we can personally do to recapture some of the love, joy, and peace of this wondrous season.

Is your Christmas Season filled…*less* with the Xploits of consumerism and…*more* with the Love of Christ? This is what Christmas Love is all about and why I think it is so precious. Wouldn't you agree?

"The cure for all the ills and wrongs, the cares, the sorrows, and the crimes of humanity, all lie in that one word "love'. It is the divine vitality that everywhere produces and restores life." ~ Lydia Maria Child

Conclusion

I hope you have enjoyed my compilation of inspirational quotes and anecdotes. The main source of my quotes is from the book titled, "The Best of Success ~ A Treasury of Ideas" compiled by Wynn Davis. This book is a lovely present that my husband and I received many years ago. As you can well imagine, it is a much cherished and well used gift. I truly love and appreciate the wisdom of others and have personally benefited from the wealth of knowledge that is found in their inspirational words.

"A Woman's Voice" ~ Volume I ~ is my voice reaching out to each of you in a soft and caring manner. These are a series of short stories adopted and edited from my blogsite also titled, "A Woman's Voice". The only exceptions are the two touching stories provided by my husband, Fred, and my daughter, Andrea. My goal in all of my written words is to touch your heart and soul in such a way that you might know true peace and inner joy no matter the circumstance. Peace and joy....beyond human understanding is one of my greatest hopes for each of you.

Please watch for "A Woman's Voice" ~ Volume II. I have every desire to share my thoughts and experiences with you. May God grant you His choicest blessings in all that you say and do. Please know that He is the strength found during our weakest moments in life. I have come to the profound realization that it has been well worth being weak…in order to recognize and embrace that Divine strength. I wouldn't want it any other way!

A Woman's Voice

~ Inspirational Short Stories ~

Volume 2

DOLORES AYOTTE

A Woman's Voice (Inspirational Short Stories) Volume 2
Copyright © 2014 by Dolores Ayotte. All rights reserved.

No part of this publication may be reproduced, stored in a retrieval system or transmitted in any way by any means, electronic, mechanical, photocopy, recording or otherwise without the prior permission of the author except as provided by Canada and United States copyright law.

Book design copyright © 2014 by Dolores Ayotte. All rights reserved.
Cover design by Dolores Ayotte
Interior design by Dolores Ayotte
Printed by CreateSpace
Published in Canada
ISBN: 978-0-9948673-2-2
Self-Help, Motivational & Inspirational

Disclaimer: The suggestions provided in this inspirational book are based on a personal point of view and not in any professional capacity.

The Human & Humane Self-Help Author

Dolores holds a Bachelor of Arts degree with a major in psychology from the University of Winnipeg as well as teacher certification from the University of Manitoba. She has also taken courses in human relationships and communication.

Her self-help books are written in retrospect based on a proven recipe, one she has incorporated step by step into her own life. Over time, Dolores eventually developed better life coping skills which inspired her to put pen to paper and write four previous books about her experiences. She utilizes quotes, anecdotes, humor, and her own personal stories when necessary to make her suggestions relevant and to give an example of how to use her simple tips in daily living.

She is now retired and spends half the year with her husband at a retirement community in Arizona. For the remainder of the year, Dolores enjoys her children and grandchildren in Winnipeg, Manitoba where she was born and raised. She continues to learn from all the people who touch her life.

Table of Contents

Introduction

1. The Inception of A Woman's Voice
2. The Feminine Spirit
3. Me, Myself, and I
4. The Coupon Queens
5. Storytelling
6. Pointing the Way
7. Embracing the Power Within
8. Reconciliation versus Resolution
9. LAFF (until your stomach aches)
10. The Stigma of Mental Illness
11. Underdogs
12. Dealing with Depression
13. Life's Journey
14. Dealing with Anger
15. Dreams
16. Childless Mother
17. Having a Bad Day
18. Forgiveness
19. Added Talent

Conclusion

Introduction

"Writing makes a person very vulnerable. It opens you to public criticism, to ridicule, to rejection. But it also opens conversation and thought. It stirs minds, and touches hearts. It brings us into contact with our souls. So how can it possibly be a waste of time, an idle act, a mistake, a betrayal of truth? Who can possibly tell us not to do it?" ~ *Joan Chittister, Order of Saint Benedict*

This quote really hits home for me. How many of us feel discouraged by the lack of response we get to what we write? How many of us have felt vulnerable by what we have written and how people might view us? How many of us have been ridiculed, perhaps even mocked, criticized, or rejected because of what we have shared? How many of us have had what we thought were friends and then they used what we have written to hurt us. Sharing our heart is similar to wearing our hearts on our sleeves…it leaves us wide open. As writers, we truly become open books. So why do we do it? I have the answer in a nutshell, at least from my point of reference. There is a niggling inside of us that just won't go away until we put pen to paper and write our thoughts. There is a deep thirst inside an author that will only be quenched by having or making the opportunity to express these inner seeds that start off so small but manage to become a book one day.

I know that I have felt several of the previously mentioned emotions. I have also known disappointment and discouragement but...I totally agree with this quote by Joan Chittister. My writing has stoked conversations outside of people's natural comfort zones. People have opened up to me and told me about their personal struggles because they know I understand and have compassion for their plight. My words have also stirred minds and touched hearts as I spur on people to think for themselves. I also encourage others to learn to love themselves in order to truly love, accept, and respect others. Believe me, this is no easy feat and not one I take lightly.

Writing is no "idle act", no "mistake", and not meant to be "a betrayal of truth". At least, not my writing anyway. Writing is a gift that has been bestowed upon me and many others like me who want to share their talent with the world. To do less or to bury this talent would be a betrayal, not only to myself but to my Maker, the One who so generously and abundantly gives us all a variety of gifts to share with our fellow humankind. Yes...sometimes it can hurt, but the rewards for our desire to share this wondrous gift usually far outweigh the negative consequences. Therefore, I salute all my fellow writers today. Chin up. Even if we positively touch only a few people with our written words, we have touched a whole world to God. I also salute those who take or make the time to read our words. Without them...we would be like a tree that falls in the forest with no one around to hear the sound of its impact. Yes indeed...as an author I have something to say. If you are an author reading my words, you know exactly what I mean. If you are a reader of inspirational books, you are honoring me beyond words by reading what is near and dear to my heart. Hopefully, what I have to share will touch your heart in a very intimate way.

You are about to read A Woman's Voice ~ Volume 2. In the first chapter I will give you a little preamble as to its inception. It will better explain why this inspirational book has been written and what you can expect if you decide to read on. At the end of most chapters, there will be a series of motivational questions. You, as the reader can opt to write down the answers or you can choose to mentally reflect upon them...either way, the key is to be honest with yourself. Personal reflection can be seen as a gentle reminder that as life goes on we have many opportunities to live, learn, and reflect on life in general. We also have every opportunity to learn from these reflections to help ensure that history doesn't repeat itself. One of my daughters recently made a poignant observation on life. She states that if we don't learn our lessons the first time around, opportunities to get it straight will keep arising until we do. Makes perfect sense to me. How many times do we get into the same kind of fix and we ask ourselves "why" we are facing these same perplexing situations over and over again. Well…in my opinion, I think my daughter has effectively answered this question. We didn't learn our lesson the first time around.

In order to add some levity to this inspirational book, I have interspersed some lighter topics in between the more serious ones. All work and no play is not nearly as much fun as a combination of them both. Wouldn't you agree?

As usual, I have utilized numerous quotes and anecdotes from both women and men alike in order to add to your reading pleasure. I prefer to draw from a wide wealth of wisdom and enjoy the sagacity of both genders. I also recommend that you read all of my books in doses, not unlike taking medicine. These motivational writings are not meant to be read in one or two sittings like fictional books and perhaps other non-fictional books. My books are meant to be digested in small doses in order to reflect upon and perhaps glean the guidance that we may need to develop skills to better cope with the challenges of life.

1 ~ The Inception of A Woman's Voice

"Remember no one can make you feel inferior without your consent." ~ *Eleanor Roosevelt*

I recently had a lovely conversation with one of my twin daughters. A few years ago, she had the wonderful occasion to attend a conference in Los Angeles, California. I could clearly hear the enthusiasm and pleasure in her voice as she described her experience to me. This was a conference for women and by women. Attendees varied in ages from, twenty-something, to a woman in her eighties. They all had a common goal...they wanted to find their voices and learn to better express themselves. In other words, they all desired the same end goal. These women wanted to be "heard".

Before I share a small part of her experience with you, I want to relate to you how she heard about this special event in the first place. My daughter is a social worker who has been a stay-at-home mother for the last several years. She has had four children in a ten year span and they keep her challenged and extremely busy. She has chosen to put her career on hold in order to meet the ever growing demands of her little family.

Before this particular conference, her husband sent her the information via e-mail giving her the heads up about this event specifically geared for women knowing that it would be of great interest to her. I chuckled to myself when my daughter told me she emailed her husband back at work to ask him "why" he would send this information to her when he knew full well that she would be unable to attend due to her busy home life and domestic demands. Guess what happened next? Her husband must have secretly wanted her to go because he helped make it happen. He took on the responsibilities of their young family for almost five days so that my daughter could benefit from this learning opportunity. She was about to experience a first time adventure by getting away alone to enjoy a totally new and exciting experience.

The presenter of this conference was speaking on a particular topic (women's voices) for the first time. Therefore, my daughter was part of the inception stage of this relevant topic by the organizer of the conference. Approximately five hundred women from all over Canada and the United States attended. In a nutshell, the theme of the conference was about the voices of women and the desire to be heard. My daughter was given this great opportunity because her husband made the choice to instinctively hear her voice and helped create the occasion for her to meet with other women in their efforts to also be heard.

In my opinion, my daughter actually already had a voice at home because her husband was instrumental in getting her to the conference. It was apparent to me that no matter what our walk in life may be, we can have the opportunity to have a voice. In other words, that voice starts in the home. Once it is heard there it can evolve into other forums as well.

Shortly thereafter, my daughter returned home a much more enlightened and contented individual. The fire was burning strong inside her with the keen desire to make a difference in this, oftentimes, troubled world we call home. Her enthusiasm lit my fire too. Yes…we all have a voice and we all want to be heard. Now, the real challenge is yet to unfold as we make every effort to find someone who is willing to listen. We often hear the expression that someone is "a gifted speaker". I have a sneaking suspicion that the seldom…if ever used expression…"a gifted listener", is nearly common as "a gifted speaker" or viewed as equally important. Trust me…it is.

"Don't compromise yourself. You are all you've got." ~ Betty Ford

"If better is possible, good is not enough." ~ *Source Unknown*

Personal Reflections:

1. Do you consider yourself to have a voice in either the work place or at home?
2. If so, are you communicating effectively and truly expressing yourself as an equal when you have the opportunity to speak?
3. Do you have the tendency to voice your opinion only when it agrees with strong-minded individuals or do you feel strong enough with your own voice and personal views to publicly disagree with others? Hint: A good example of not feeling comfortable with your views is having the tendency to discuss them afterwards with a friend or co-worker whom you know will agree with you and your take on things.

2 ~ The Feminine Spirit ~ Andrea Ayotte Cockerill

"A strong woman knows she has strength enough for the journey, but a woman of strength knows it is in the journey where she will become strong." ~ Source Unknown

A woman's voice...

What does she sound like? She is fierce, intuitive, and powerful, for she is aware of her own relevance. Her knowledge runs deep, fueled with the passion coming from the women that have come before her. She looks into the eyes of the little ones around her knowing that if she denies her worth, she denies the worth of the next generation of femininity to come.

She has experienced the deep personal pain of having ignored the whispers of her own soul, or when she has had the courage to speak up and then quickly backing down yet again. She sees the women around her struggling as well, many overeating to try to temper the power within.

Others may spend too much money or try to portray perfection, or they may devalue the role they play in the lives of their families and communities. Just maybe if these women could keep their minds busy enough, they won't see where they have either given up their voices or where they have been taken from them.

At last, she knows the courage it will take to speak her truth as she can no longer sacrifice her spirit. When she felt that her voice was irrelevant, she cared that others did not hear her. Now she feels her relevance deep within her soul and no longer seeks out the confirmation that it is worth something…that she is worth something. There is a deep freedom in honoring and celebrating the fierceness that resides in the inner voice of a woman.

It is this power that if collectively used, will create deep and everlasting changes for the world we live in and for the generations to follow. She thanks the women before her, who have used their strength and wisdom to make it easier for her, and she uses the next generation as an inspiration to continue to find the courage to stand tall.

"You have to accept whatever comes and the only important thing is that you meet it with courage and with the best you have to give." ~ Eleanor Roosevelt

"We are what we repeatedly do. Excellence, then, is not an act but a habit." ~ Source Unknown

Note: The previous article was written by my daughter who I mentioned in The Inception of A Woman's Voice, the first chapter of this inspirational book. The questions I am about to add are my own.

Personal Reflections:
1. Is your voice fierce and intuitive or shy and reserved?
2. Do you feel that you have a powerful position in life whereby you can influence others and feel good about it?
3. Do you consider yourself to be a positive person?
4. Are you comfortable in your own skin?

3 ~ Me, Myself, and I

"There is an infinite difference between a little wrong and just right, between fairly good and the best, between mediocrity and superiority..." ~ *Orison Swett Marden*

I have a nickname given to me by my husband. It is Bob. Many years ago, one of my grandchildren started calling me Bob. She was learning how to talk and for whatever reason, when she saw me, the name Bob popped out of her mouth. Perhaps she was trying to call me Baba and it lovingly came out as Bob. Over the years, my husband has formed the habit of teasing me and calling me by that very name. I don't mind at all as it brings back such fond memories of a very precious time in my life.

It has been my observation that at times in life, it is very easy to dwell on ourselves and not look around at the people in our lives and what they are up to or what they stand for in terms of their beliefs. Many times over the years my husband and I have come to use the expression it's "all about Bob" to describe when either one of us becomes too self-focused or self-absorbed. We also tend to say this when we notice that we have lost some of our objectivity. It is very difficult to not fall into the trap of being very interested in what's going on in our own lives and not interested enough in what's going on the lives of those around us. We've observed that we are not alone in the ability to engage in this not-so-attractive behavior.

Personally, one of my pet peeves in life is to be in a relationship that is one-sided and off balance. I neither want to offer this to my friends nor do I expect to receive it from them. If we become "all about Bob" people or if we hang out with "all about Bob" people we soon become disenchanted with the friendship. My goal in life is to strive for balanced relationships where we are both interested in what is going on in each other's life.

I must admit that I no more want it to be all about someone else than I want it to be all about me. Relationships are about relating to each other. It's not about some lopsided pseudo friendship whereby one gets to talk and the other gets to listen most or all of the time. What fun is that? In my opinion, this kind of relationship won't stand the test of time because if it's too one-sided and eventually one or the other will get emotionally tapped out or just plain frustrated with the lack of reciprocity.

I realize that there may be times in a person's life when they may need a compassionate ear or require more support;

however, if it is usually this way even during the good times, the relationship is doomed to fail from the onset. We all have needs and they must be fulfilled in varying degrees in order for a true and long lasting friendship to unfold. I have no desire for people to look at me and think I am an "all about Bob" personality. However, I can honestly say that I don't want to always be in the audience either or what I have come to refer to as someone else's personal fan club.

I want a healthy balance when it comes to the friendships in my life. I have no desire to play "show and tell" and not take a turn. I already did that when I was an elementary school teacher. It may not be necessary for it to be fifty-fifty all of the time, but as previously stated, there does have to be some reciprocity in order to feel validated in any long term quality relationship.

Once again I stress that I have no desire for it to be all about me, myself, and I, but on the other hand the reverse also holds true. I don't want it to be all about you, yourself, and yours each and every time we get together. In my opinion, it is no better to be always "giving" than it is to be always "taking" in any relationship. There has to be a happy medium in order to feel satisfied.

Life is a matter of give and take and this concept works best for most people.

"Yesterday is a cancelled check; tomorrow is a promissory note; today is the only cash you have so spend it wisely." ~ Kay Lyons

Personal Reflections:

1. When you are sharing a conversation or communicating with a friend, do you do more than your fair share of talking or do you listen more?
2. Would you consider it to be a balanced relationship? If not, is it what you really want or are you settling for less in order to not ruffle any feathers and keep the status quo?
3. Is it okay to want balance and equality in your friendships? Do you feel more fulfilled in this type of relationship?

4 ~ The Coupon Queens

"People seldom improve when they have no other model but themselves to copy after." ~ Goldsmith

It seems so much easier to admit some of our silly, little habits when we find people who operate much the same way. My mom was one of the biggest coupon people I know. She loved cutting out coupons and taking them to the store to redeem them for cash. The stores weren't nearly so sticky all those years ago and they would dole out cash for your coupons whether you bought the product or not. My mom loved this little practice because money was tight in those days and this coupon money ended up being her extra cash to spend the way she saw fit.

I'm a coupon clipper. There's no getting around this fact. The other day when I went to the local pharmacy with my wallet full of coupons, I got a bunch of excellent deals. When I jumped into the car and looked in the mirror, I realized I had become my mother. Oh my, I could hardly believe it. I not only look like her, I'm now doing the same darn thing. The scary part about it is that the realization crept up on me in such an unexpected way that it brought a smile to my face.

I don't really need to engage in this habit. I'm not in the same position my mom was all those years ago, so why do I do it?

I'll tell you why. I have a group of friends that I socialize with and guess what? We all do the exact same thing. It's actually hilarious. It's a wonderful game that we all seem to enjoy. We go shopping and to restaurants with our handy coupons. Buy one meal, get one free has been the deciding factor in many of the restaurants we frequent. There is even a half-price day at the local movie theater. Our husbands have started to be as hooked as we are and they are cooperating to the fullest extent. Usually you can only purchase one item per coupon, so the guys sometimes join us so that they can use a coupon too. You know how much these men like to go shopping but yet somehow or other we get them to come along with us so we can benefit from two coupons instead of just one.

As I'm writing this and trying to describe this habit of ours, it makes me want to burst out laughing. Here we are…all excelling in the art of being thrifty. We are so proud of our bargains. When we're gone and leave our children their inheritance, if there's any to be had, I'm sure they'll spend it faster than you can "shake a stick" and probably without a moment's hesitation. We've had a blast saving our money. Hopefully, our children will have as big a blast spending it. What do you think?

"Every job is a self-portrait of the person who did it. Autograph your work with excellence." ~ Source Unknown

Personal Reflections:

1. Do you have any quirky little habits?
2. Do you see how we form some of these habits based on past experience or from those who have influenced us in some of our past decisions?
3. Do you ever look in the mirror and can hardly believe who you are and what you've become?
4. Every experience is a learning opportunity…try not to forget that your children and grandchildren are observing a lot more that you might think. What kind of an example are you setting for them?

5 ~ Storytelling

"To live is so startling it leaves little time for anything else." ~ *Emily Dickinson*

It brings me great pleasure to elaborate on my philosophy of my love for storytelling and the motivation behind the desire to share my humor, my true life experiences, and my innermost self. I delight in sharing the stories of others as well, in order to better get my points across or to enhance the lives of those who want to vicariously benefit by listening and learning from those who have gone before them.

Our telling one another's stories can be a means of extending not only their reach in touching other people's lives, but our own hand as we reach out to help others attain their full potential as followers of Christ. As a result, we are in the process of learning to strive together to attain our true aspirations and capabilities as human beings. In doing so, we help each other achieve this desired common goal to become the "Body" of Christ on earth.

In helping others, we ourselves, are being helped. The mutuality of the relationship forms the foundation of all that we are as Christians. When we grasp each other's hand in this way, we form a circle of God's love and create the chain of His Divine Essence as we link up with like-minded individuals.

It is the combination of reaching out and reaching back that binds us together in the most profound way. It is the fabric that knits us together as humankind.

"You may not be responsible for your heritage, but you are responsible for your future." ~ Source Unknown

Inspirational poem

"No vision and you perish; No ideal and you're lost;
Your heart must ever cherish some faith at any cost.
Some hope, some dream to cling to, some rainbow in the sky,
Some melody to sing to, some service that is high."
~ Harriet Du Autermont

Personal Reflections:

1. Do you find that you understand a concept better if an example or a story is used to better explain it?
2. When a story is shared with you, can you or do you mentally relate to it at times?

3. Do you find comfort in knowing that similar situations have occurred in your own life?
4. Is there comfort in knowing you are not alone?
5. When people listen to your stories or life experiences, does it bring you comfort when they can relate to your situation?

6 ~ Pointing the Way

"To succeed is nothing-it's an accident. But to feel no doubts about oneself is something very different: it is character." ~ Marie Leneru

At times, I know that I have a somewhat different philosophy on life than other individuals. I have always considered myself to be a teacher even before I had formal credentials. Although I left the classroom many years ago, the classroom has never left me. I feel like I am now very much "a teacher without walls". When I did teach elementary school, we used to have "show & tell" on a regular basis. The children loved this little practice, as I am sure they still do to this day in many classrooms around the world.

I think the children enjoyed when another child had a story to tell but I think they especially enjoyed when they had something to show. This visual aid made their story all the more enjoyable. As teachers, we also had a little saying that goes something like this. Tell me and I forget…Show me and I remember…Involve me and I learn. It has been my experience that telling someone what we think or believe may not always leave the mark we want it to. Showing them by leading with our example may have a greater impact and others will probably get a better idea of our message. Involving these individuals in what we are trying to teach will indeed have the greatest effect.

One of the things I have come to realize is that when we involve others, it is also necessary to know when to get out-of-the-way so that they can see the path clearly ahead. A good teacher needs to know when to "back off" and let the student forge ahead on their own. If we are constantly pointing the way, we could very well be hampering the student's line of vision and future learning experiences. Therefore, at some point, we may actually be doing them more harm than good.

Part of being more than a good teacher is knowing when to stop teaching and "let go...let God". The time when good teachers become great ones is when we figure this out. Do you know when to "back off" when necessary or "teach" when needed? It is no easy feat to discern. Therefore, being the most effective teacher may be a task similar to doing a balancing act or walking a tight rope. It's a slippery slope to say the least.

There is also a very fine line between what is seen as preaching versus teaching. Preaching may have a negative connotation if it isn't done in the right setting. We must be in tune, not only with ourselves but with those around us, in order to achieve the best results. Effective teaching usually has a way of positively involving others. I'm not so sure that preaching is seen in this same light. Preaching by our peers can be seen as a lot about telling and very little about showing or involving. Being told what to do or how to behave doesn't always achieve the desired positive results. We all have the opportunity to teach or to preach in our everyday lives. What I'm suggesting, is that we take a moment and ask ourselves how we're coming across.

"For every failure, there's an alternative course of action. You just have to find it. When you come to a roadblock, take a detour." ~ *Mary Kay Ash*

"Life is my college." ~ *Louisa May Alcott*

Personal Reflections:

1. Do you agree that there is a difference between teaching and preaching?
2. Would you agree that a sermon at church would be considered preaching?
3. When a friend/family member is sharing their experiences with you for your benefit in order to

help you better cope with your possible problems, would you consider this to be a form of teaching?
4. Do you agree that both teaching and preaching can be beneficial but they each have their place?
5. Would you agree that both teaching and preaching must be handled very carefully in order to not "talk down" to others? In my opinion, relating to others by sharing our similar experiences and how we coped helps even out the playing field. What are your thoughts on this?

7 ~ Embracing the Power Within
Andrea Ayotte Cockerill

"I am only one; but still I am one. I cannot do everything, but still I can do something; I will not refuse to do the something I can do." ~ *Helen Keller*

The other day I had an epiphany but it wasn't the kind of epiphany that makes one feel great and connected to God. It was the kind of awakening that actually brought me great sadness for its truth could not be denied. In many ways I have tried to feed a hunger inside myself with things that could never fill the gnawing feeling this hunger created. I have tried many times to search deep within, looking for answers that may comfort its emptiness. Maybe if I could fit in on the outside by measuring up to societies outward markers, I wouldn't feel so lonely on the inside.

I have come to understand, with great sadness, that at some level my loneliness comes from my own hunger of wanting to belong yet feeling like somehow I have fallen short of this goal. I had previously concluded that if I was special in some outwardly way then maybe that elusive gift of feeling this sense of belonging would be within my grasp.

What a painful feeling it is to feel like there is nothing particularly special about who you are, just because you are you.

My instinct is to distract myself from such uncomfortable sadness but by learning to run and face its shadow, the power it holds lessens. As its power lessens, my own sense of who I am increases which is something I am no longer willing to sacrifice. I have decided to stand in this shadow of distorted thinking and embrace its lessons. Soon I will be able to see that my specialness is derived from just being created in the image of God and that nothing else on my part needs to be done to gain the sense of belonging that I desire.

May you too find your own courage to look deep within to claim your own power and to celebrate your specialness that's always been there simply because you were created with love.

Inspirational Poem

    As I stretch towards the center of you,
    in silence I find the space that exists between the mind and the heart,
    and I am reminded that there is nothing to fear.
    Nothing can separate me from this place of comfort.

But in order to reach it,
I must pass through a moment that lies just between letting go
and the moment I grab hold of you.
It is my faith that bridges this divide.
When I reach you it becomes clear.
All I was ever meant to do, forever and for always, was to love myself.
All I was every meant to do, forever and for always, was to love you.

~ Andrea Cockerill

"He who loses wealth loses much; he who loses a friend loses more; but he that loses courage loses all."
~ Cervantes

Note: Once again this article was written by my daughter who I mentioned in the first chapter of this inspirational book. The chapter referred to is titled The Inception of A Woman's Voice. The questions I am about to add are my own.

Personal Reflections:

1. Do you ever feel lonely?

2. Do you sometimes even feel lonely when surrounded by people? In other words, is it possible to feel alone in a crowd?
3. What do you do to overcome these feelings?
4. Do you consider yourself to be special? If so...why? If not...why not?
5. Do you have a difficult time seeing your self-worth? If so...re-read the previous poem. Hint: Learning to love yourself as you are is one of the keys.

8 ~ Reconciliation versus Resolution

"The cure for all the ills and wrongs, the cares, the sorrows, and the crimes of humanity, all lie in the one word 'love'. It is the divine vitality that everywhere produces and restores life." ~ Lydia Maria Child

A while back I read an article that mentioned the difficulties a family had experienced before and after the death of their mother. The author of this article went on to say that she prayed for things to be resolved amongst her siblings and herself. The answer from God wasn't quite what she expected but regardless of this fact, in the end she felt that her prayers were answered nonetheless. Reading this article motivated me to have a look at my own life and my personal ideas about resolution and reconciliation. Is there a difference between the two concepts and if so what is it? Before further discussing this topic, I decided that the best course of action was to look up the exact meaning of these two words in the dictionary.

One definition for the word resolution that I found in a well-known dictionary is *"the power to make choices and set goals and to act upon them firmly in spite of opposition or difficulty"*. Another definition is *"unwavering firmness of character or action"*. Yet another is *"the quality of mind enabling one to face danger or hardship resolutely"*. When I look at one of the meanings to the word resolution I interpret it to be a strong belief or take on a certain situation that others may not agree with. More than likely the resolute person recognizes this fact and will act on their convictions regardless of the opposing view. I think that once we are resolute in our position, we may become unwavering no matter the consequences. One of these consequences may very well be choosing to stand alone. To me, the key words are *"to make choices and set goals and to act upon them firmly in spite of opposition or difficulty"*. In deciding this course of action, we become resolute in our beliefs and actions regardless of the outcome. It is truly having such a strong belief in our own convictions that we are prepared to, not only stand behind them, but also to stand alone in acting on them.

When I looked up the word reconciliation in the same dictionary, I discovered that there were also several definitions. The meaning that stuck out the most was *"to bring something into a state of agreement or accord"*. After careful consideration, I would have to say that reconciliation/agreement is not always attainable in every conflicting situation. Perhaps, the initial noble goal in any disagreement is to try to achieve a reconciliation whenever possible but if an agreement cannot be reached, then the next step is to try to zero in on a compromise in order to resolve the situation. However, if this option doesn't pan out, a responsible resolution to any given problem may very well be to choose the concept of "agreeing to disagree" in a respectful way. In reality, neither party is prepared to bend. I think that the writer of the previously mentioned article was alluding to this fact with her family. Obviously, they were not going to agree, but no one was willing to compromise on their stand. In other words, it was a stalemate. However, by "agreeing to disagree" in a loving way, they resolved their problematic family situation to her satisfaction. Therefore, God did answer her prayers and she was grateful for this fact.

In truth, this woman admits that she had been praying for reconciliation with her family in the hope that they would all agree. This did not happen. In the end they resolved the situation by rising above their differences; albeit, this was not her first choice. However, the only possible answer to her prayers obviously was what unfolded between the family members. This type of resolution means being open-mined enough to accept that reconciliation is not possible for the parties concerned. The best course of action is to just accept this fact and move on with life in a respectful and civil way. Resolution does not change anyone's stand. Resolution at its best, is the sincere and meaningful decision or act of "agreeing to disagree" without rancor. In my opinion, if there is still rancor, the issue is not really resolved. It is merely beneath the surface waiting for another occasion to rear its ugly head. It takes much courage to face such disagreements head on and to deal with them intelligently, maturely, and without any negative residual consequences. This goal is no easy feat to be sure.

"Choice, not chance, determines destiny." ~ Source Unknown

"The scar that you acquire by exercising courage will never make you feel inferior." ~ D.A. Battista

Personal Reflections:

1. Do you believe in the term irreconcilable differences? Personally…I do.
2. If you do too and you realize that you are never going to agree on a certain point of view or way of acting, do you try to deal with it head on or do you try to avoid confrontation?

3. If you face the problem head on and come to the conclusion that you have arrived at a stalemate and you are never going to agree, what would you consider to be a reasonable course of action?
4. For me...not all disagreements are deal breakers, what about you? What I am basically saying is that some areas of disagreement are more serious than others. In other words, some can be overlooked depending on the situation and others cannot. It is up to the individuals involved to make that decision.

9 ~ LAFF (until your stomach aches)

Do you enjoy doing any kind of puzzle fun like Crosswords, Four Squares, Cryptograms, etc.? I personally engage in solving a variety of puzzles and word games including Jigsaw Puzzles, Word scraper, Scrabble...I love them all!

I am fascinated by the English language and how rule oriented it is on one hand and totally not on the other. We all know how phonics works and how you can sound out words. Sometimes it is as easy as pie and other times it doesn't make one ounce of sense because there are so many exceptions to the rules.

One such word that catches my attention is the word LAUGH. Why isn't it just spelled like it sounds...LAFF? Do you want to know why I much prefer this version?

At times when I struggle in my relationships with other people, I spell it this way. It's kind of like an anagram for me and perhaps you can use it as one for yourself too as you have a closer look at life.

L – Love

A – Accept

F – Forgive

F – Forget

When someone has either purposely or unintentionally offended me, if I learn to LAFF, then I can genuinely LAUGH it off and better enjoy my life. A well-developed sense of humor can really enhance life. You may have to work at it, but it is well worth the effort. LAFFTER really is the best medicine!

Personal Reflections:

1. Have you really learned to LAFF in life? Do you know that until we engage in this form of LAFFTER at the deepest level, it is very difficult to achieve inner peace and contentment?

2. Do you know that in order to truly LAFF with others, it is necessary to learn to LAFF with ourselves first? In other words, we must love and accept who we are and then learn from and forgive ourselves for our past mistakes. If we learn to "not be" so hard on ourselves by recognizing our own human frailties, we will be more compassionate and understanding toward others. Last but not least, it is wise to forgive and forget the offensive behavior;

however, try your best to not forget the lesson learned otherwise history may repeat itself.
3. Have you honed your sense of humor? Do you take things too seriously? Once again I repeat, have you learned to LAFF at yourself?

10 ~ The Stigma of Mental Illness

Memories are the key not to the past, but to the future. I know that the experiences of our lives, when we let God use them, become the mysterious and perfect preparation for the work He will give us to do." ~ *Corrie Ten Boom*

Over the last several years I have had the opportunity through my writing and publishing of books to personally share my efforts to deal with depression and other forms of mental illness. I was prompted to write my inspirational books for basically two reasons. I am a depression survivor. I know the despair and debilitating effects of major depression. The reason I refer to myself as a survivor means I have figured out ways to effectively deal with overcoming my depression. It took not only months, but years, of dogged determination to move past this illness. Even despite my success, I still have to face the cyclical periods it poses and deal with this illness when it creeps up.

I am grateful to say that I have lived a full and rewarding life despite this baffling condition. I consider myself to be very fortunate because the initial prognosis by the medical professionals was not very optimistic. In my early thirties, I was told that I would be on medication for the rest of my life. I flatly refused to accept this course of action. I have worked long and hard to come up with better life coping skills and I have succeeded. It's not to say that I never get depressed, it's only to say that I am better able to handle the situation when I do.

The other reason I am writing this chapter is that it coincides with the above quote. My experience with depression has enabled me to *"become the mysterious and perfect preparation for the work"* God has planned for me. I feel that I am being called upon to be an advocate to share my experiences so that others will be encouraged to speak more freely about theirs. In this way, perhaps the "stigma" attached to mental illness will continue to decline. My heart has gone out to people who have shared some of their stories with me. As a result, I would like to share some of these stories with you. Dealing with mental illness is never easy whether you are the person suffering with the symptoms or the family members and friends supporting the mentally ill individual. This heart wrenching story explains more.

One anonymous acquaintance says… *"After more than 14 years of symptoms, I finally couldn't let my mother go untreated anymore. We had been trying to get her to go for voluntary treatment for years. I had her committed against her will and after a 6 month stay in a mental facility she is* now staying with my brother who makes sure she takes her medication. She was diagnosed with Schizophrenia, but because it took so long for treatment to start, she will never be the same person she was. She lives in her own world now and is unable to communicate in any significant way with people. I would love to see the perception of general public change towards Schizophrenia. Most people believe that it gives the person suffering from it split personalities and that they hear voices and that they are all homicidal. Truth is Schizophrenia is characterized with 'hallucinations' of all the senses, sight, hearing, touch, taste, but it also breaks down the person's ability to interact in social settings. My mother was smart enough to hide the worst of the symptoms from us for many years. If the 'acceptability' of mental illness was better, she might not have tried hiding it."

Another anonymous acquaintance states… *"Undoubtedly there are many people who still bear a stigmatizing attitude towards mental illness, some of whom may even direct that towards certain sufferers they encounter. That is sad. However, I'm sure that there are many other people who do not have that negative attitude or mindset, and yet fail to encourage and show acts of kindness, because they don't understand the sufferer's needs. They don't want to offend, or are afraid that their words or attempts at kindness may offend and 'set (the individual) off,' and result in rejection. My wife and I have experienced this during our years of pastoral ministry. However, we learned through repeated exposure and experience to look and care beyond the episode of the moment."*

Personally, I think education and public awareness will eventually help individuals to show more compassion and empathy towards those with mental health issues. The care givers also need the support and encouragement of others because they are deeply affected as well.

"Expect trouble as an inevitable part of life and repeat to yourself the most comforting words of all: "This, too, shall pass." ~ Ann Landers

"The mind, like a parachute, functions only when open." ~ Source Unknown

Personal Reflections:

1. Do you or does anyone close to you suffer from any form of mental illness?
2. Is the illness out in the open in a similar way that one might be open about a physical illness?

3. If you are having an "off" day or dealing with bouts of depression, do you try to hide it from others? If so, why?
4. Do you feel there is a stigma to having a mental illness?

11 ~ Underdogs

Little minds are tamed and subdued by misfortune, but great minds rise above them." ~ Washington Clark

Have you ever considered yourself to be an underdog? Although I have internally referred to myself as an underdog many times, I'm not quite certain that I know exactly what this expression means. Instead of going into a big diatribe about what I think it means, I just want to use it in the sense that actually applies to me and my life. In past publications, I've already described that I had poor and simple roots as far as my background is concerned. My parents were not well-educated, although nor were many of their peers. I don't want to say that I was born on the wrong side of the tracks, but I'm sure there were some people who thought that's exactly where I lived in my youth.

I remember the mother of my closest childhood friend telling her daughter that she didn't want her to play with me. You know what little children are like, they repeat things verbatim. My friend, who was an only child, didn't hesitate to share this information with me. I came from a family of six children and we didn't live in the most desirable neighborhood. There was a single mother on welfare next door to us living with her nine children. There were other kids in the area who were always up to some kind of mischief. Some of the boys would get into pretty serious trouble and a few of them ended up in reform school for juvenile delinquents. Mind you, by today's standards with all that is going on with drugs and gangs etc., what these boys were up to is probably what the police would now consider to be "small potatoes". My dad was pretty strict with us as children but there is no way that he could have prevented any of us from seeing and knowing what was going on in the neighborhood. I was sixteen years old when we moved to another more upscale area of the city, so I had already developed what I consider to be my "street smarts".

If there is one thing I remember when I was young is that I never looked down on anybody. Perhaps it's because even as a child there were some people already looking down on me. I instinctively never wanted to make another person feel the same way I did when this happened. There wasn't one person I would ever consider to be less than me or not good enough to be my friend…not even those mischievous neighborhood boys.

As I go down memory lane and revisit that very house I grew up in, it no longer holds the negative stigma it once did when I was young. The street is much improved with some houses being torn down and replaced by much nicer ones. It actually looks quite lovely now.

I think one of the best things about being a child is having the innocence to see things in such a lily-white way that we think everyone views the world the same way we do. It's only after we experience the full gamut of life, that we can allow ourselves to openly admit some of our negative experiences. We can become quite jaded if we don't learn from our past. In order to better enjoy our lives, we must make every effort to get past our negative life experiences and learn to look at life from some of our innocent childlike perspective. It's a pretty hard goal to achieve, but I can tell you that it is not impossible. I must admit that it does require a concentrated effort and a lot of work to try to get back some of the little pleasures that we may have enjoyed as children.

"Your living is determined not so much by what life brings to you as by the attitude you bring to life; not so much by what happens to you as by the way your mind looks at what happens." ~ John Homer Miller

It's neat how much information we processed as children and how much we stored in the recesses of our mind. I'm pretty sure you're no different than I am. Parents, whether mine, yours, or your friends are very influential in forming the values, self-image, and self-esteem of young children. Children in their own innocence readily pass along this information. In retrospect when I have a glimpse of it now, I was somehow or other taught to believe that I was less than some of my friends. This is why I came to describe myself as an underdog. It took me a very long time to realize that I was equal to others and that my friends are my peers.

My friend's mother would have been a much kinder person if she took these sage words of advice into consideration... *"As long as you keep a person down, some part of you has to be down there to hold him down, so it means you cannot soar as you otherwise might."* ~ Marian Anderson

Also... *"Never forget that life can only be nobly inspired and rightly lived if you take it bravely and gallantly, as a splendid adventure in which you are setting out into an unknown country, to face many a danger, to meet many a joy, to find many a comrade, to win and lose many a battle."* ~ Anne Besant

Personal Reflections:

1. Have you ever felt as if you were less or not equal to another human being? If so, why?

2. Did another person try to make you feel less than them or look down on someone else in your presence?

3. If so, what did you do about it?

12 ~ Dealing with Depression

"Challenges are what makes life interesting; overcoming them is what makes life meaningful." ~ *Joshua J. Marine*

As expressed earlier, depression is a very complex thing and it has the tendency to touch most of our lives in one way or another. I have read that depression is anger turned in. From my own personal frame of reference, I have come to believe that this can be a true statement depending on an individual's circumstances. Having said that, I have also come to realize that figuring out what we're angry about can be a real challenge.

At times, we become very angry at ourselves and what is going on in our lives. We can also become angry at other people because we may want to blame them for our depressed state or our overall unhappiness. Perhaps our anger is a result of hurt feelings and what other people have said or done to us or what they aren't doing for us. There is a natural tendency to let this anger fester inside so that it becomes so much bigger than it actually is. Our own feelings or depression actually end up feeding, these oftentimes, perceived hurts and resentments.

When we aren't enjoying our lives the way we think we should, we may become frustrated and resentful. We can often think it is someone or something outside of ourselves that is causing us to feel this negative way. Even if the harm that has been done to us is very real, it is very difficult to let go of because it has become such a part of our basic being. In essence, this state of depression or negative life cycle can become like a trusted friend that we rely on as we visit these not so positive feelings over and over again.

It's as if these "down" feelings become comfortable and, at times, we can end up isolating ourselves from other people because they may not feel the same way about our situation as we do. We think that we understand ourselves so much better because we know what has been done to us and what we feel inside. These inner feelings are okay for a time as we work through the healing process and try to better help ourselves but if we stay in this state too long, they can become our true enemy. There is a fine line.

Making the effort to get past the anger in this negative life cycle is a huge decision. It means that we have decided to let go and to move on in a positive direction. It means that we have decided to forgive not only those who have added to our grief, but to also forgive ourselves. It means that we have now taken back the responsibility for the happiness in our own lives. I can assure you that this decision is not for the faint of heart. *"You must do the thing you think you cannot do." ~ Eleanor Roosevelt*

We must look in the mirror and decide to act. This is a very crucial point in the healing process. It is the very first step in deciding that we truly want a happier self. It's taking back our own personal power. It's realizing that we are accepting the responsibility for the majority of happiness or unhappiness in our own lives by adjusting our own attitude and choices in life. *"The best thing about the future is that it comes one day at a time." ~ Abraham Lincoln*

There will be steps forward and steps back but in the end if we make up our minds to endure, we will climb this uphill battle and succeed.

I want to stress once again that this is a very crucial decision. It is much more natural to feel like the victim of someone else's bad behavior towards us than it is to grow up and admit that our own slate may not be as sparkly clean as we perceive it to be. It means we must embrace the fact that we may very well have had a hand in what is happening in our lives. It might explain why we lack confidence, self-esteem and may be adding to our own depressed state. Yuck…who really wants to look at themselves in such an analytical way? If we really want to move up the ladder and onto happier times, we must make a momentous decision and take a very big step. This step is what I refer to as the "leap of faith" step because we are also deciding to reach out to a Higher Power and get past these not-so-good feelings about ourselves. You are not alone. Reach down really deep, and there's a hand inside you that will reach back and together you will find the strength, the courage, and the inspiration to move on up so you can better see the light of day.

Winning the battle over depression, will be one of the biggest victories you will ever make in this game called "life".

I know…I've been there.

"Quality is never an accident. It represents the wise choice of many alternatives." ~ Willa Foster

Personal Reflections:

1. Have you ever felt depressed?
2. Do you know what the symptoms of depression entail?
3. Do you believe that you can just "snap out" of a depressed state?
4. If you or someone else you know suffers from depression what is your usual course of action? In

other words, how do you handle it? Do you share your "down" emotional state or do you try to hide it?

13 ~ Life's Journey

"Great minds must be ready not only to take opportunities, but to make them." ~ Colton

Many years ago I decided to take responsibility for the unhappiness in my life and I made several life style changes. One of the biggest and best decisions I ever made was to get on a more regular exercise routine. Although I was fairly young, I never really had much time to dwell on myself because I was busy raising my family and working outside the home as well.

In order to get my life back on track, I decided to begin walking on a regular basis. I started off small by walking in between my bus stop connections on my way home from work instead of merely standing at the bus stop to wait for the next bus. After I built up my stamina and my desire to walk, I would not catch the first bus that came along opting to walk a little farther each day.

Walking brought so much pleasure to my life that I proceeded to increase my distance so that eventually I was able to walk home on some days...a distance of 6 miles. I started this program over twenty-five years ago. I don't think I could even do the math to figure out how many miles I have walked thus far nor calculate the unbelievable benefit I have received from this simple decision so many years ago. I have met several people along the way and enjoyed the company of many other walkers. I still walk three miles every week day and continue to enjoy all the friendships I have made in this special way. At times, it is very difficult to make time for ourselves with the very busy schedules that we all have. However, when we succeed in doing so, in the end everyone benefits. Walking is so simple yet so beneficial. Taking the first step, may very well give you such positive results that you will want to take many more subsequent steps.

Regular exercise of any kind is definitely a good habit and has many other positive side effects. Exercise is very therapeutic in dealing with and managing stress.

"Happiness is not a state to arrive at, but a manner of traveling." ~ Margaret Lee Runbeck

Personal Reflections:

1. Do you endeavor to make time for yourself each day?
2. Do you have a regular exercise routine?
3. Do you sacrifice your own needs in order to meet the needs of others? If you do this, how do you feel about it? When this happens, more often than not, inner

resentment will build up and eventually affect how you view life. In other words, life will seem negative instead of positive.

4. Make time for yourself no matter how busy you are...what can you do to enhance your life as far as exercise is concerned?

14 ~ Dealing with Anger

Every situation properly perceived, becomes an opportunity." ~ Helen Schucman

I have often expressed the view that depression could be a result of anger turned inward. There are many reasons why a person might experience depression but this is merely the one that I am choosing to focus on again in this inspirational book. In my opinion, there is also a genetic predisposition to depression but I won't be discussing that view in this chapter. If interested, I have gone into great depth in one of my other publications **Up The "Down" Ladder** which deals with many of my views on depression as well as some simple ideas to help overcome mild to moderate depression. At times, I have the opportunity to hear the views of others concerning this subject. Some are more willing to share these views than others; however, most prefer to do so based on anonymity. One such comment comes from a personal contact with the pseudonym of Hope. She prefers to remain anonymous and I am honoring her wishes. Her comment inspired me to address the anger issue which most of us face at one time or another in our lives. Being angry is a choice. It is not to say that at times in our lives, we don't have the right to be angry. However, we can choose to admit the emotion we are dealing with and eventually decide to move on to a more positive and upbeat frame of mind. I would like to take this opportunity to share Hope's point of view as she so eloquently speaks on the emotion of anger.

This is the comment almost in its entirety:

"I agree whole wholeheartedly that moving past anger is a decision. Sometimes I think the things that are at the root of our anger are out of our consciousness... I had a very wise person once tell me that when the reason is out of your consciousness, you are still a victim of it. But once you are aware and still acting in the same self-destructive way, you are no longer a victim...you are choosing to be that way and blaming someone else. I think her point was, once you are aware of the self-destructive behavior, then you are wholly responsible for moving on or not. No longer is there room for blame. So that took me a while to digest, but I think now, that it is very true.

It's amazing how powerful you feel, once you realize there is a choice to be angry or not. Simple solution...very difficult to live by. With a daily commitment to think otherwise, there is proportional reprieve of the burden in that day."

I was extremely moved by Hope's insight concerning the subject of anger. I read it over and over again to get the full scope of its meaning. It also made me do more soul-searching and inspired me to write more on the topic of anger. I know a person who has suffered from severe depression for many years. This person has been on a heavy regiment of medication for depression and although it helped somewhat, it never totally eliminated the depressed state.

After many years of suffering, a therapist finally managed to help her get to the bottom of her severe depression. Through counselling and extensive therapy, she was able to finally peel back the layers of what was causing her deep and, often times, debilitating depression. What appeared to be the main cause, although there were other factors, was what she perceived as the consistently bad behavior of her husband throughout their well over thirty years of marriage. After this realization, her depressed state turned outward with the expression of anger toward her husband. Her anger toward him was so great that eventually they had to go their separate ways. Over a span of several years, what was bottled up inside her and coming across as depression was in actuality, extreme anger. In essence, it appeared to be her inability to identify and accept what was really going on in her marriage and effectively deal with it. I don't know if it was a combination of her inadequacy and/or her reluctance to address the real issue but it certainly came back to haunt her marriage. One thing I do know is this…the consequences of her suppressed anger were devastating. This is merely just one case which demonstrates that depression can be a result of anger turned inward. By not facing the reality of her situation sooner, the challenges became too great to overcome and the damage to her marriage was irreversible.

A few years ago in my reading travels I came across these words of wisdom. The source is obscure but the words are well-worth repeating… *"if you are angry, there are three ways you can approach the emotion: express the anger, suppress the anger, calm the anger. Expressing anger in a controlled manner, is a healthy approach. However, this approach is often difficult to do because it involves a balancing act — getting your needs met without hurting others. In short, controlling anger involves respecting both yourself and other people, especially those who are the cause or object of your anger, while still being able to express it. The second approach is suppression. Suppressing anger can backfire. When a person tends to suppress his anger, he can develop high blood pressure, hypertension or even depression. The last approach is calming the anger down. A person who is able to calm his anger down is able to control his outward behavior. However, if he is unable to calm down, he may hurt someone or even himself."*

I very much agree with the author of these words. What is said makes perfect sense to me and perhaps to you too. As you can see it is no easy feat to deal with anger; however, it can have many devastating negative, emotional, and physical consequences if we don't. No matter what...we all experience anger now and then, it is whether we effectively deal with it in a healthy way or not that leads to either a positive or negative result.

"Getting something done is an accomplishment; getting something done right is an achievement." ~ Source Unknown

Personal Reflections

1. Do you agree that we all experience anger at one time or another?
2. Do you consider anger to be a healthy or unhealthy emotion?
3. How are you dealing with your anger? In other words, do you express it or suppress it? Do you feel that you are able to express it in a

controlled manner in order to get your point across or do you "lose it" by engaging in uncontrollable outbursts?

15 ~ Dreams

"Some people dream of worthy accomplishments, while others stay awake and do them." ~ *Source Unknown*

"To be what we are, and to become what we are capable of becoming, is the only end of life." ~ *Robert Louis Stevenson*

At times, we don't always realize the importance of our dreams. To me, the ability to dream and to have hope go hand in hand.

To dream is to look ahead and aspire to be more than what we are at the present moment.

To dream is to have the desire to make a difference in this world we call home.

To dream is to be able to look forward and to try to achieve a goal that is new to us or that we thought was unattainable. To accomplish our dream is to realize that our lives are worth living. In doing so we gain self-worth, self-respect, and in most instances the respect of others. This occurs especially when we have gone against the odds and risen above what appears to be the impossible. When we dream, we have hope. When we have hope, we have a reason to live. Our "raison d'être" is the essence of our being. Without it, we don't have much. With it, we have an indomitable spirit that drives us to broaden our horizons and soar with the eagles.

"There is only one thing for us to do, and that is to do our level best right where we are every day of our lives; to use our best judgement, and then to trust the rest to that Power which holds the forces of the universe in His hand..." ~ Orison Swett Marden

"In the moment that you carry this conviction...is that moment your dream will become a reality." ~ Robert Collier

Personal Reflections:

1. The dreams I am referring to in this short chapter are what I consider to be personal aspirations. Do you aspire to be more than you are?
2. Are you able to look down the road at your life and set goals and aspire to accomplish them?
3. Do you give up too soon or do you make every effort to succeed in your personal attempts at greatness?

4. Do you allow the negative opinions of others to deter you in your efforts to pursue your dreams?

16 ~ Childless Mother

Nothing strengthens the judgment and quickens the conscience like individual responsibility." ~ Elizabeth Cady Stanton

Quite a few years back, my husband and I returned from a brief trip to Swift Current to attend our granddaughter's Confirmation. She had chosen her grandpa to be her sponsor. What an incredible honor bestowed upon him. When he received our granddaughter's phone call, I witnessed his pleasure first hand. We hadn't visited with our daughter and her family for several months and we saw a huge change. The girls had grown and matured and as usual we enjoyed our short visit with them.

As was the norm, on our way home in the car we listened to the local radio station to get a bit of news about the surrounding area. The talk show on this particular morning was about an unfortunate car accident that had taken place on March 29, 2009 in a small town just outside of Swift Current.

The topic immediately grabbed our attention because two of the mothers that had lost their daughters in this accident were being interviewed on the car radio about this tragic event. Three young girls, two sixteen years of age as well as a fourteen year old, were making a left turn on the highway when a car driven by a seventeen year old male tried to pass them on the left side. He was driving at 128k/hr. when he collided into their car. All three of the girls died in this horrible car accident. The mothers, the families, and the friends of these young women have been beside themselves with grief over their loss.

The young man happened to be sentenced the week before this radio talk show and the discussion revolved around the punishment he received and whether it was adequate enough. Although the judge gave him a sentence to suit his age when the accident occurred, by the time of the trial he was eighteen years old. Some people called in to express their opinion by stating that he did not receive a long enough sentence for the crime committed.

My heart goes out to the mothers who lost their daughters in the prime of their lives and in such a tragic way. Both of the mothers being interviewed were compassionate and open-minded despite their unbelievable loss. However, comments were made by some callers citing that this young man had his whole life to live while the girls had so sadly lost theirs by his reckless actions. Others felt that he did not show enough remorse.

Later on in the talk show, I briefly heard a comment from another caller who probably knew the boy's family. She stated that the young man was struggling with his life. My heart immediately went out to him and his mother as well. Unless this man has no conscience at all, I cannot fathom that he has been unaffected by having had a hand in the death of these three young women.

I would have to think that he will somehow or other be scarred for life. He lives in a small town where he will have little or no anonymity. He will live with the reality of his careless actions for the rest of his life. He will probably marry one day and have children of his own. He may very well learn to pray and appreciate the quality of life when he faces his actions as a more mature individual.

Yes, those young girls, their families, and their friends got robbed; however, I personally do not envy the life that this young man now has to live. Anyone who thinks it is going to be easy is only fooling him/herself. I also feel a sense of compassion for this young man, his family, and his friends. I'm sure his mother's heart is aching because there is much more to face in her son's life and he will need the support of them all.

They all lost so much that fateful day and their lives are forever changed. Three mothers lost the lives of their daughters on March 29, 2009 and one mother lost the innocence that her young son can no longer enjoy. All four mothers lost children that tragic day. Only now, one will be haunted by his reckless actions for the rest of his life.

"There are many truths of which the full meaning cannot be realized until personal experience has brought it home." ~ John Stuart Mill

Personal Reflections:

1. Have you experienced personal loss whereby you hold another person responsible for that loss?
2. Is it an easy feat to forgive someone who has so carelessly taken from you?
3. What are the consequences if you don't? In other words, who are you hurting if you harbor anger and resentment?
4. Give yourself the time to heal but in the end the best remedy is to "let go, let God". Do you think that by tapping into your faith, you will be more able to forgive the offender?

17 ~ Having a Bad Day

"Take each day and relish each moment. Take each bad day and work to make it good." ~ Lisa Dado

"If you get a second chance, grab it with both hands. If it changes your life, let it. Nobody said life would be easy, they just promised it would be worth it." ~ Source Unknown

I want to share a cute little story with you to demonstrate how simple it is to turn your life around one step at a time. Many years ago when I was working downtown in a major mall, oftentimes, I would go shopping during my lunch hour. This mall consisted of many businesses, retail stores, restaurants, and pretty well everything working people might want at their fingertips.

On this particular day, I was having one of my "off" days. We all have these kinds of days now and then, but this one was particularly bad. As mentioned in some of my earlier chapters, I suffer from depression and I could sense that I was headed in that direction if I didn't take positive action. I decided I would go for a walk in the mall because I wasn't what one might consider to be "good company" in this rather foul mood of mine.

As I was walking along, I was wondering what I could do to cheer myself up and make for a better day. When I finally reached a section of the mall that had an outside door, I noticed a somewhat bedraggled man sifting through the sand in one of the big ashtrays near the entrance to the mall. There was no smoking allowed in this huge underground facility so anyone that came through the door had to "butt out".

It was obvious to me that this poor man was searching for the longest butts in the ashtray so he could have a few good puffs. By the way he was dressed and by his actions, it was apparent to me that he could not afford to buy his own cigarettes. Just looking at him and what he was doing made me forget all about my woes and my bad day.

As I focused on him a light bulb went on in my head and I decided to do a good deed or a random act of kindness. Over twenty years ago, to my knowledge no one referred to these acts by that term, but it doesn't mean to say that they weren't happening just the same. I went up to this man and gently asked him to wait right where he was standing. He looked up at me and nodded his head in agreement.

I turned around and went into a nearby drugstore and bought a large package of cigarettes and some matches. This was a time when smoking wasn't as nearly frowned upon as it is today. After purchasing the cigarettes, I quickly walked back to where the man was standing and handed him my recent purchase, receipt and all. I didn't want anyone to think he had stolen the cigarettes should he be seen with them. I suggested that he enjoy his gift and perhaps share them with some of his friends. He was very pleased, but what he said after that, changed my mood for the whole day and many days afterward.

This was a Monday, and Mondays can be kind of blue at times, just as it was for me that particular day. When this less fortunate man thanked me for the cigarettes, he quickly added, "What are you doing next Monday?" I almost laughed out loud because I found his question so surprising and somewhat amusing. He completely caught me off guard. He was planning on meeting me there as often as possible, perhaps every Monday if I was willing. It was such a cute response. I couldn't help but smile at him as I told him that this was just a spontaneous, one time occurrence and I just wanted to make his day.

In essence the exact opposite happened, he made mine instead. By reaching out to someone with a greater need than my own and giving in such a small way, it made me realize that it truly is better to give than to receive. I was given so much that precious day because even after all these years, the memory of that incident still brings a smile to my face. By doing what I did, I discovered that *"no one is in charge of your happiness but you"*. ~ *Regina Brett*

This little story reminded me of how fortunate I really was and how by going out of my way to make a less fortunate person have a good day, it actually ended up creating a better one for me. You really cannot give away a kindness in life.

The pleasure that this man had on his face was a hugely rewarding experience. He was very grateful and he thanked me for my kindness. However, it was me who had every reason to thank him for accepting my simple gift and getting me out of my funk. He was the one being kind and gracious. He did not get offended by my gesture. He made me smile and managed to elevate my mood by showing his gratefulness that blue Monday so many years ago.

"You may be dead broke and that's a reality, but in spirit you may be brimming over with optimism, joy, and energy. The reality of your life may result from many outside factors, none of which you have control. Your attitudes, however, reflect the ways in which you evaluate what is happening." ~ *H. Stanley Judd*

Personal Reflections:

1. Do you ever have bad days?
2. If so, what do you usually do about it?
3. Have you created simple, little ways to help get yourself out of your "funks" before a deeper depression sets in?
4. Do you engage in random acts of kindness?

18 ~ Forgiveness

Be kind and compassionate to one another, forgiving each other, just as in Christ God forgave you." ~ Ephesians 4:32

I love this biblical quote. It demonstrates to me that I am to forgive others "just as" Christ has forgiven me. Perhaps, I see things a little differently than some other people when it comes to forgiveness but I would like to take this opportunity to explain my views. I know it has been said that we will not be forgiven "until" or "unless" we forgive others. However, according to the above biblical quote, I believe that I can also go to God as a sinner and seek forgiveness for myself from Him. When I experience His generous gift of forgiveness and mercy, I then learn to forgive others in the same way that I have been forgiven. In other words, I am emulating God's forgiveness, "just as Christ God forgave" me.

I believe God set the ultimate example of forgiveness by dying on the cross for my sins and I have the option of going humbly before Him and accepting His forgiveness. He's the ultimate Teacher, not me. I personally need to learn from the Master. It's not me showing God how I forgave so that I may be forgiven, but rather, it is God showing me how to forgive by first forgiving me for my sins and indiscretions so that I can go on to forgive others who have wronged me.

In my situation and perhaps in other's as well, by following His holy actions I am better equipped to forgive others because I have learned from the greatest Forgiver of all times. When we accept Jesus as our personal Savior, we not only want to forgive, it becomes a way of life as we follow in Jesus' footsteps and forgive others as we have been forgiven by God Himself. In essence, I have chosen to first look at my own sinfulness, human weaknesses, and need for forgiveness. I have made a conscious choice to do this instead of looking at how others have wronged me and my need to forgive them in order to be forgiven by Christ. Once I see my own weaknesses and ask for God's forgiveness, I am better able to accept the weaknesses of others and forgive them theirs. The above biblical quote as well as the following one helped inspire my interpretation on forgiveness...forgive each other "as the Lord has forgiven you".

"Bearing with one another and, if one has a complaint against another, forgiving each other; as the Lord has forgiven you, so you also must forgive."

~ **Colossians 3:13**

This third biblical quote by Matthew says it a little differently…more like the "until" or "unless" or "if" description of forgiveness that some other people might use to describe what a sinner must do to be forgiven.

"For if you forgive men when they sin against you, your heavenly Father will also forgive you." ~ *Matthew 6:14*

Perhaps, either way we choose to look at the power of forgiveness, whether we repent and seek it, or whether we forgive others then seek it…if we end up at the foot of the Cross, we are ultimately forgiven our transgressions. I don't think the act of forgiveness is about drawing a line in the sand or an "either/or" type of concept. It's not about if you don't do things the way I think they should be done, then it's the wrong way. It's also not about trying to force people to think like we do or by expressing that somehow or other we are closer to God than they are. Our relationships with God are very personal because we are all unique individuals. With that in mind, it is wise to acknowledge that each relationship with God is as unique as our personalities. Therefore, it is necessary to respect each other and trust that God has a plan for each of us even if it is a bit different from someone else's path. Our heavenly Father has taken our uniqueness into consideration when forming our relationship with Him and

He knows exactly how to draw us closer to Him. For that, I am eternally grateful!

Personal Reflections:

1. Do you know anyone who tries to get you to share their religious views?
2. How do you view this behavior?
3. Do you engage in this type of behavior yourself...that of trying to get others to think like you?
4. Have you considered that actions speak louder than words?
5. The best way to get people to believe in Christ is to set the example so that people will want to emulate you. Do you agree?

19 ~ Added Talent

The following four stories have been penned by my sisters at my personal request. They have generously agreed to share their talent with my reading audience and I am delighted.

The first story is written by my oldest sister, Shirley Gauthier Sarafinchan who has also agreed to let me use some of her many beautiful pictures for the covers of my books. I am publishing each of their stories according to their birth order in our family to demonstrate a sense of fairness and equality amongst us as a family. Linda Briscoe is the third daughter after me with Lorraine Gauthier and Gloria Korell being the youngest girls in the family. We also have a brother, Ron Gauthier, who is the eldest adult child and only son.

I enjoyed each of the stories provided by my sisters as they reflected on cherished moments in their lives. I thought, you as my readers, would enjoy them as well.

Thank you to my sisters and also to each of you for honoring us by reading this inspirational book.

The Old Farmhouse

Shirley Gauthier Sarafinchan

This poem was originally written on April 30th, 1981 about an old farmhouse that was once home to a family but sometime later I associated it with abused women. In essence, it reminded me of women who strive so very hard to make homes for their families. No matter how hard they try, they are worn down and battered. Finally they have the opportunity and the strength to stand up for their rights and to free themselves from their bondage to at last find the peace and solace that they so richly deserve. The old farmhouse is a symbol of a refuge for abused women.

THE OLD FARMHOUSE

Amid the fields it stands so alone, so serene, so peaceful, yet filled with an emptiness all its own, this old farmhouse that was once called home.

Its shingles torn and tattered, windows scarce of glass, doors hanging by a single hinge alas this old farmhouse so battered.

What secrets dare to lie within its walls, love, laughter, fun and joy, echoes of little children running down the halls, tears, sorrow and pain for loved ones lost?

Music must have filled the nights with sounds of crickets and birds in flight, the sweet scent of the prairie harvest and wild flowers a pleasant sight.

The tantalizing aroma of freshly baked bread reaching every corner of the old farmhouse and early morning sunrises filling each room full of light, the warmth from the wood stove soon to spread.

Memories fill this old farmhouse, nothing more is really left but, it has served its purpose in this life and now alone, it can be at rest.

Remembering When
Linda Briscoe

When I was a child we walked to school on the very first day! Brand new outfit and school bag, packed with crayons and all new supplies. I walked and walked for what seemed like forever, happy to finally be at school, only to realize that there would be the same walk home at lunch, then back to school and home again!

The days would be glorious in the fall, still warm enough for just a sweater. The leaves would start to fall to the ground and the winds would pick up. Before I knew it, the cold would be in the not too distant future. It was time to bundle up to make the walk to school as bearable as possible. Now, in the bitterness of winter, lunch bag packed, off to school I went. Bundled tightly, with my scarf around my forehead and neck, I braved the long walk to school. Oh…it could get bitterly cold, so cold as the wind blew through my not so warm coat and the well-worn boots which had known other winters. Is this cold winter ever going to pass?

Then it changed. The days started getting longer, the sun started getting stronger, and I was very excited as I could spot the first patch of pavement. The ditches were so inviting filled with melting ice and water. Trusting to step on the now thin ice and not sink…only to find a boot full of water was merely a fine line away…just one more step and a little more pressure before the ice cracked and I could feel the SPLOOSH as the cold water seeped into my boots. A young child and a ditch full of water are like two magnets being drawn to each other.

On that walk home from school, the snow was only going to bring the worst of spring, with its dirty snow banks and slippery sidewalks after a cold night. Getting splashed by a passing car was the norm as I surged forward on my long walk home. Try as I might to keep my spring coat clean and the runners that I changed into after school as I rid myself of my heavy rubber boots was an impossible feat.

Through the Eyes of a Child
Lorraine Gauthier

As children, with the purest of hearts we see life with wonder. We learn to walk by crawling, standing, and falling...so similar to life as an adult. We educate ourselves by seeing, hearing and copying those we want to be like...a parent, an older sibling, or a friend.

We all started off as children and somewhere in us, we still have the heart of that young child. I know I still do. As an innocent child, I usually chose to do things for the absolute right reason. At age two, I chose to cut off my hair to look like a boy. The reason...my dad had 'hoped' I was a boy because he wanted another son after my brother and three sisters were born. I loved him and wanted to please him. I wanted to give him what I 'thought' was a boy, as if cutting off my hair would do the trick.

Years later, we had another girl born into our family. Now there were five girls. We had a small house and had to learn how to share. We were lucky to get a new chest of drawers. This was very exciting to me because now we could each have our own drawer for our personal belongings. However, I was worried that we, as sisters, wouldn't recognize our own drawer. I decided to engrave our names on each drawer so that my sisters knew which one was theirs. Needless to say, this was not well received. My dad was furious. I was punished because I had damaged the new chest of drawers

How many times in life, even as an adult, do we have perfectly good intentions, with the purest of hearts, yet it is received differently? I am grateful that throughout our lives we can still have the heart of a child. Over the years, this child's heart will feel both joy and pain. It truly becomes our guide to how we perceive things as an adult. Hopefully, we can continue to see the beauty in all things like we did as an innocent child!

Siloam Mission

Gloria Korell

In the past few months I had the privilege of volunteering at Siloam Mission with my daughter Meagan. I experienced firsthand what it was like to do "God's work". Observing the volunteers, people of all races and ages, working in such harmony to provide for the patrons of Siloam gave me the impression the work was effortless. The eagerness to prepare a meal and clean up afterwards with such smiling faces and cheery hearts delivered a strong message about the rewards of giving.

My first visit to Siloam left me with a different opinion of the homeless. I discovered that they could be one of us and we could be one of them and as my volunteer experience continued so did my connection with these people. We so often take for granted our blessings in life. In the weeks following, each time I visited Siloam the rewards became greater. In a strange way I was becoming "addicted". I needed to feel the "high" from giving. It felt like I was becoming needy myself. I wanted to continually hand over that plate of food so I could hear the thank you or see a smile on someone's face.

Yes, the significance of people needing one another. My need was just as great as theirs. As a result, this experience has been one of the most rewarding in my life and I am grateful my daughter had the opportunity to open her heart and give to others less fortunate. All our experiences in life help us to "connect the dots" on our journey. For me, this experience not only opened my eyes, but also my heart and it made me realize that I too was being fed.

CONCLUSION
~ New Endings~

How many times in life do we live with regrets? We look back and sometimes our lives haven't gone quite the way we hoped for or expected. We get so disappointed and discouraged with ourselves, our lives, and with the people around us. No one can change the past, not even God. What's done is done. The key to living a peaceful life is to not let the past affect our present or future happiness.

There's nothing wrong with looking back and learning from our past mistakes but rather than mourn the loss of what could have been, we can choose to start now to make a new ending. By doing so, we can change the outcome of future events. Our lives can hold a much brighter future when we look ahead with faith and courage.

Faith in God and a renewed faith in ourselves...because we have taken the time to look in the mirror and realize as well as capitalize on the personal power that we possess in order to start now and create a new, more positive, and acceptable ending to our lives. Go for it! Life is too short to wake up with regrets. So love the people who treat you right. Forget the ones who don't. believe everything happens for a reason, a season, or a lifetime.

A Woman's Voice

~ Inspirational Short Stories ~

Volume 3

DOLORES AYOTTE

A Woman's Voice (Inspirational Short Stories) Volume 3
Copyright © 2014 by Dolores Ayotte. All rights reserved.

No part of this publication may be reproduced, stored in a retrieval system or transmitted in any way by any means, electronic, mechanical, photocopy, recording or otherwise without the prior permission of the author except as provided by Canada and United States copyright law.

Book design copyright © 2014 by Dolores Ayotte. All rights reserved.
Cover design by Dolores Ayotte
Cover photo by Shirley Gauthier Sarafinchan
Interior design by Dolores Ayotte
Printed by CreateSpace
Published in Canada
ISBN: 978-0-9948673-3-9
Self-Help, Motivational & Inspirational

Disclaimer: The suggestions provided in this inspirational book are based on a personal point of view and not in any professional capacity.

The Human & Humane Self-Help Author

Dolores holds a Bachelor of Arts degree with a major in psychology from the University of Winnipeg as well as teacher certification from the University of Manitoba. She has also taken courses in human relationships and communication.

Her self-help books are written in retrospect based on a proven recipe, one she has incorporated step by step into her own life. Over time, Dolores eventually developed better life coping skills which inspired her to put pen to paper and write four other books about her experiences. She utilizes quotes, anecdotes, humor, and her own personal stories when necessary to make her suggestions relevant and to give an example of how to use her simple tips in daily living.

She is now retired and spends half the year with her husband at a retirement community in Arizona. For the remainder of the year, Dolores enjoys her children and grandchildren in Winnipeg, Manitoba where she was born and raised. She continues to learn from all the people who touch her life.

Table of Contents

Introduction

1   Old Black Thumb
2   These Boots
3   Peace in Life's Simple Pleasures
4   Two Wrongs
5   Genetics and Depression
6   My Oxygen Mask
7   Dysfunctional Mother/Daughter Relationships
8   Storage Bins
9   Taking Notice
10   The Three Faces of Eve
11   Spit It Out
12   On Being Tested
13   Objections Anyone…
14   The Weather Channel
15   Early Bird
16   Sadness
17   The Art of Playing Cards
18   The Persistence of the Spirit
19   Leadership
20   A New Word to Make you Smile

21 Driving Miss "D"
22 Change
23 Live…Laugh…Love
24 My Phantom Tooth
25 Common Courtesy
26 What's Eating Gilbert Grape
27 Self-Acceptance and Regrets
28 And the Winner is…Not Me!
29 Extraordinarily Ordinary
30 Savor the Flavor

Conclusion

Introduction

A Woman's Voice ~ Volume 3 is the last book in this three part series. I hope you enjoy reading this inspirational book as much as I've enjoyed writing it. Once again, I have included some guest writers who have agreed to share their thoughts with us. My daughter Andrea Cockerill has written several stories in Volumes 1 & 2 and is featured again in Volume 3. My husband Fred Ayotte is also featured in Volume 1 and now again in Volume 3. As usual, I have utilized numerous quotes and anecdotes from both women and men alike to add to your reading pleasure. I prefer to draw from a wide wealth of wisdom and enjoy the sagacity of both genders. I also recommend that you read all of my books in doses, not unlike taking medicine. These motivational writings are not meant to be read in one or two sittings like fictional books and perhaps like other non-fictional books. My books are meant to be digested in small doses in order to reflect upon and perhaps glean the guidance that we may need in order to better cope with the challenges of life. On the whole, the majority of the stories in Volume 3 are short and easy to read.

I would like to take this opportunity to thank Fred, Andrea, and Shirley for both their past and present contributions to the success of A Woman's Voice. As you can see by this lovely cover, a photo generously provided by my talented sister Shirley Gauthier Sarafinchan, the reflection in the water can be seen as a gentle reminder that as life goes on we have many opportunities to live, learn, and reflect on life in general. We also have every opportunity to learn from these reflections to help ensure that history doesn't repeat itself.

"Writing makes a person very vulnerable. It opens you to public criticism, to ridicule, to rejection. But it also opens conversation and thought. It stirs minds, and touches hearts. It brings us into contact with our souls. So how can it possibly be a waste of time, an idle act, a mistake, a betrayal of truth? Who can possibly tell us not to do it?" ~ *Joan Chittister, Order of Saint Benedict*

The above quote is very fitting and really hits home for me. It is found in the Introduction of A Woman's Voice ~ Volume 2 and is well worth repeating in Volume 3 as it applies to all my writing. I could not possibly express this message in my own words any better than Joan Chittister. At times, I feel the need to admit that I have also been discouraged. I, too, have felt vulnerable and affected by other people's views of me. Other times, I have been both criticized and rejected because of what I've shared. I've even had a few of my friends use what I have written to hurt me. When people have access to our innermost selves, this information can, at times, be used in unkind ways. Sharing our heart is similar to wearing our hearts on our sleeves…it leaves us wide open. As writers, we truly become open books. So why do we do it? I have the answer in a nutshell, at least from my point of reference. There is a niggling inside of us that just won't go away until we put pen to paper and write our thoughts and bare our souls. There is a deep thirst inside an author that will only be quenched by having or making the opportunity to express these inner seeds. They may start off so small but manage to grow into a book one day.

I repeat that I have known disappointment and discouragement but…I totally agree with this quote by Joan Chittister. My writing has stoked conversations outside of people's natural comfort zones. People have opened up to me and told me about their personal struggles because they know I understand and have compassion for their plight. My words have also stirred minds and touched hearts as I spur on people to think for themselves. I also encourage others to learn to love themselves in order to truly love, accept, and respect others. Believe me, this is no easy feat and not one I take lightly.

Yes...writing is no "idle act, no "mistake", and not meant to be "a betrayal of truth". At least, not my writing anyway. Writing is a gift that has been bestowed upon me and many others like me who want to share their talent with the world. To do less or to bury this talent would be a betrayal not only to myself but to My Maker and the One who so generously and abundantly gives us all a variety of gifts to share with our fellow humankind. Yes...sometimes it can hurt, but the rewards for our desire to share this wondrous gift usually far outweigh the negative consequences. Therefore, I salute all my fellow writers today. Chin up. Even if we positively touch only a few people with our written words, we have touched a whole world to God. I also salute those who take or make the time to read our words. Without them...we would be like a tree that falls in the forest with no one around to hear the sound of its impact. Yes indeed...as an author I have something to say. If you are an author reading my words, you know exactly what I mean. If you are a reader of inspirational books, you are honoring me beyond words by reading what is near and dear to my heart. Hopefully, what I have to share will touch your heart in a very intimate way.

"Courage is the price that life exacts for granting peace." ~ *Amelia Earhart*

1 ~ Old Black Thumb

"I have learned that success is measured not so much by the position one has reached in life as by the obstacles he has overcome." ~ Booker T. Washington

When I wrote my first book, ***I'm Not Perfect And It's Okay ~ Steps to a Happier Self***, I quickly stated that I was "no author" in the introduction. Some people may find this a strange comment coming from a person who was in the processing of publishing a book.

At that time, my goal was to reach out to people to help prevent them from experiencing what I had been through with my bouts of serious depression. I was simply a greenhorn when it came to any kind of writing, so therefore, I didn't claim to be an author. I merely considered myself to be a person reaching out to help others. I wanted to touch as many lives as possible and I didn't know any other way except by the written word.

My gardening fame falls into much the same category. I'm "no gardener" but I sure have been trying all my life to be one. My husband can attest to this fact because he appears to be right there by my side. Although, he claims he is "no gardener" himself, the two of us persist in our endeavor to be the best at maintaining our backyard so it can be as picturesque as possible.

As the years have gone by, I know that at some point we crossed the line and can probably now call ourselves gardeners. The term old black thumb that my son-in-law first teasingly called me when he observed my lack of gardening skills, may no longer apply. He has now admitted that I'm actually better at it than he initially thought me to be. The proof is in the picture. I now have evidence to prove it.

I kind of feel the same way about my writing. I may have started off by stating that I was "no author" but with perseverance and dogged determination, I must admit I'm fast becoming one.

"I do not think there is any other quality so essential to success of any kind as the quality of perseverance. It overcomes almost anything, even nature." ~ John D. Rockefeller

Personal Reflections:

1. Do you have a hobby or engage in an activity that you know you could be better at?

2. Do you stick with it until you achieve a level of success that you are satisfied with or do you give up too soon? In other words, do you persevere in attaining a certain level of satisfaction?
3. Do you compare yourself to others or do you treat yourself as the unique individual that you are and make every effort to attain your own personal goals according to what you are capable of?

2 ~ These Boots

"The spirit, and the will to win, and the will to excel are the things that endure." ~ *Vince Lombardi*

Some of you may have already read the book I referred to in the previous chapter, therefore, I am not going to go into too much detail about the content. I just want to share with you one of the first small steps of many more steps to come that helped me turn my life around. In this motivational book, I state that it is very hard to motivate ourselves when we have little desire and even less energy to do so.

Many of us have been there. There is something inside us that tells us things just aren't quite right. We want to be right with ourselves and right with the world. There is an inner discontentment that sits in the pit of our stomach which affects our zest for life. It is extremely difficult to get past this malaise because we hate the way we feel about ourselves, our jobs, and many other aspects of our lives. We have no idea how to remedy the situation or where to start to get ourselves on a more positive track. In the end, we can actually hate ourselves because we don't or can't understand what is wrong with us. We may reach an all-time low and once we do, there is only one way to go and that is up.

I recommend this suggestion based on my own experiences. Start by one small step at a time…one small accomplishable step in the right direction. I started by actually taking physical steps by beginning a daily walking routine, one block of walking, day after day until I built myself up to three miles a day. That was over twenty-five years ago. It was the best decision I've ever made in helping myself get out of the pit I found myself to be in. I got off the bench in life and became a player. I took charge of my own life and decided to make a difference. It worked. I sang this song as I walked, "these boots are made for walking and"…that's just what I did! I had to help myself. There was no other way! My dad often used this expression, "The Good Lord helps those who help themselves!" It's very true. Just try it and you'll find out for yourself.

"The journey of a thousand miles begins with a single step." ~ Miyamoto Musashi

Personal Reflections:

1. Do you find yourself down in the dumps more often than you think is healthy for you?
2. Does this feeling of ennui trickle into other areas of your life?

3. Do you have a sense of peace or do you struggle with finding contentment in your life?
4. Do you agree that starting with one small easy step could help turn your life around?

3 ~ Peace in Life's Simple Pleasures

"For fast-acting relief try slowing down." ~ Lily Tomlin

So many people have touched my life in such a positive and inspirational way that I want to share some of their beliefs and ideas with as many people as possible. This is an example of one of life's simple pleasure.

A dear friend of mine sent me a very simple message not too long ago. *"How are you enjoying spring? I have been spending long days outdoors working in the yard and cleaning up the gardens for summer. I hear the birds singing and busily eating at the feeders, and wonder, who needs radios and cell phones when there is so much to enjoy in the natural world all around us? What peace there is in just melding into the world around you and doing ordinary things and realizing that...this is as good as it gets!"*

When I first received this little message, my imagination took me into my own garden and how I feel when I am there. In the spring, as I clean up my garden with the help of my husband, I feel the exact same way.

I get so lost in the wonder of it all that the work I am doing doesn't feel like work at all. I look in awe as I see the bushes and trees bud and turn green almost right before my eyes. I watch in amazement as I notice new growth sprout from the soil after a long cold winter. I gaze at the birds and listen with pleasure to their sweet songs as they go about their daily routine. I see the empty nests in our trees and bushes and I know a new season of life has begun.

I have a little garden sign in one of my flower beds which reads "Life Began in a Garden". Every time I read this sign, I am reminded of how close I am to Our Creator as I cultivate this little piece of earthly heaven that I call home.

"You must be the change you wish to see in the world." ~ Mahatma Gandhi

Personal Reflections:

1. Do you enjoy life's simple pleasures?
2. If so, which ones are they and how do you show your appreciation and gratitude for them?
3. Do you ever give any consideration to the adage "less is more" in order to take advantage of creating less stress in your life by merely taking more time to wake up and smell the roses?

4 ~ Two Wrongs

"There is no right way to do the wrong thing." ~ Harold S. Kushner

My dad used to have one of the neatest sayings. It's been over twenty years since he passed away. I still miss him and the impact he had on my life to this very day. He was not a well-educated man nor was he perfect. I certainly remember thinking he was when I was a young child. You know how little girls can idolize their fathers. Well, I was no exception. I had such an innocent love and high regard for him that I had him on a pretty high pedestal. It took me well into my adult years to fully realize that my dad was human just like the rest of us. I used to think he could do no wrong. I spent plenty of time listening to him and the stories he had to share. He also had quite a few cute sayings. One of them that has come to mind many times over the years is "two wrongs don't make a right". I'm sure he didn't coin this phrase but it sure felt like he did.

I can't count the number of times I heard him say this adage throughout my life. When people hurt us, we have the tendency to want to hurt them right back. There seems to be a trait in our human nature that likes to get even. As I write this, there is something that happened to me to make me think of these words of wisdom. Not all people are kind and it's very difficult to be kind to people who have shown unkindness toward us. Today is a day when I need to remind myself to be kind to these people. This is when I can hear my dad loud and clear, "two wrongs don't make a right". To be unkind toward someone who has hurt me will never make things right. I will be no further ahead than the person who was initially unkind to me. Yes…my dad may not have been the best educated man in the world nor was he perfect but just the same, he sure had plenty of wisdom.

It's neat how God works to get us the messages that we need to hear if we are in tune to His communication and open to this concept. Before I went to bed I wrote this little story because I was upset. I needed to remind myself to be kind no matter what. Drawing from my memory bank, I was able to hear my father once again remind me about acceptable behavior in order to better deal with those who may have hurt me. I guess we need to hear things more than once. At times, it is also beneficial to listen to the messages outside of our own thoughts and prayers. It may give us the clarity and vision that we are seeking. God works through people and by being open to their ideas and voices of wisdom, we can also find answers to our prayers and the inner peace we are striving to attain.

"The person who pays an ounce of principle for a pound of popularity gets badly cheated." ~ Ronald Reagan

Personal Reflections:

1. Do you take the time to analyze your situation or do you react too quickly?
2. Do you see yourself as trying to pay people back for their unacceptable behavior?
3. Do you agree with my dad that "two wrongs don't make a right" or do you desire to seek revenge for wrongdoings committed against you or yours?
4. If so, do you feel good about it when you've wronged the offenders liked they've wronged you? In other words, does it make you feel better or worse?

5 ~ Genetics and Depression

"Most of the important things in the world have been accomplished by people who have kept on trying when there seemed to be no hope at all." ~ Dale Carnegie

Over thirty six years ago I gave birth to twin daughters. I didn't even know I was having twins until the day I went into labor. You can well imagine our surprise as well as our delight. Our two-year old daughter was equally delighted with her two new baby sisters. Soon after I gave birth, many people asked me if twins ran in my family. I answered…"not to my knowledge". Shortly thereafter, I heard from extended family members that there were indeed many sets of twins on both sides of the family. I only discovered this fact later on in life because now this information had more relevance to my particular situation.

In several of my books, I've discussed the topic of depression. I have briefly touched on the premise that depression can be anger turned inward. Today, I am going to discuss another opinion I have about depression. I am not a medical professional. This is only a personal opinion based on my own experience with this debilitating condition.

Perhaps, you have already been exposed to the word "predisposition". This is the word I am going to use to elaborate on what I refer to as a genetic link to depression. We have already heard, when referring to the medical model, that certain physical illnesses are genetically linked like heart disease, cancer, high blood pressure, and so on. Due to this genetic link we might be more apt to get or inherit these diseases from our ancestors. I think that a similar analogy can also be made with other illnesses like depression. When I suffered my severe bout with depression in my early thirties, I had a better look as to why I had this illness when many of my peers did not. This realization was similar to when I gave birth to twins. I subsequently learned that many of my family members had also suffered or were still suffering from a range of mild to moderate and sometimes severe depression in a similar way to me. When this debilitating illness became more relevant to me, I had a better look. In doing so, I discovered that there seemed to be a genetic link to my illness because there was a long list of family members who shared my plight.

I came to the conclusion that one of my genetic weaknesses had to do with my family history of depression. I now refer to this as my "genetic predisposition" to this particular condition. To me, it is no different than any other genes that we might inherit. In my opinion, having this "predisposition" does not necessarily mean that we will suffer from depression or other forms of mental illness. What it does mean is that we might have the propensity to the perils of depression if a traumatic event occurs in our lives to "trigger" an episode. Such traumatic events may include the after effects of combat, the death of a loved one, divorce, job loss, financial woes, stress, etc. Some of these events are impossible to control and can have a devastating effect on those with a "predisposition" to depression.

According to depression expert, Nancy Schimelpfening in her article "Depression Causes" published in December, 2011...*"The causes of depression are not entirely understood, but are thought to be multi-factorial. Studies indicate that depression is, at least in part, an inherited condition involving abnormalities in neurotransmitter functioning. Although inheritance is an important factor in major depression, it does not account for all cases of depression, implying that environmental factors may either play an important causal role or exacerbate underlying genetic vulnerabilities."*

In a perfect world where there are no traumatic events, possibly there would be no depression. I don't know. However, I do know that this is not a perfect world.

Although, we have no control over our genetic make-up, in a lot of instances we do have some control over the "triggers" that may cause our possible depression. From my personal frame of reference, this was what I have strived to achieve in overcoming my own depression. What I am basically saying here is this. If you suffer from symptoms of depression, the best course of action is to try to figure out what is causing it. This is the first step. After that, you may just succeed in figuring out what to do about it. If the "triggers" are within your power to control or avoid, your depression may also be managed more effectively if you make a conscious effort to avoid these situations whenever possible.

"When you reach the end of your rope, tie a knot in it and hang on." ~ Thomas Jefferson

Personal Reflections:

1. Do you have a genetic predisposition to depression or other forms of mental illness?
2. If so, do you take the necessary precautions to ensure that you protect yourself from possible triggers that will exacerbate your condition?
3. If you are aware of what the triggers are that negatively affect your condition, do you feel that it is

your personal responsibility to take care of yourself and prevent depressive episodes?

4. Do you agree that this is not an easy feat and that it might be necessary to seek professional help, reach out to a supportive loved one, or find a support group to help you avoid this negative life cycle?

6 ~ My Oxygen Mask

"Setting a goal is not the main thing. It is deciding how you will go about achieving it and staying with that plan." ~ Tom Landry

Not too long ago, I was listening to a talk show on the radio. I had turned on the radio expecting to hear music and instead there was a discussion going on about the joy found in being a Christian. My ears perked up and I couldn't help but listen more carefully as the guest speaker described what he thought it was like to be a Christian. He went on to say that God is supposed to come first in our lives which, by the way I fully agree with, family and friends are supposed to come second…and then we as individuals are supposed to come third. He then stated that we have been put on this earth to serve others.

Based on my religious education I know that some people may believe this to be true but I also know that it is a hard ideal to live up to. I want to be realistic about myself as a human being. I know that with all my human weaknesses and frailties, I am not always able to put others before myself and my own needs each and every time. I have also come to realize that this teaching is not always meant to be so cut and dry and by putting myself last, I may not be obeying what God has in store for me as one of His followers.

I remember working with a gentleman who told me a story as he watched me trying to adhere to the rule of serving others. I wasn't even aware that he was observing me in this way. One day while discussing business in his office, he reminded me of the oxygen masks on airplanes and how to properly use them. He was a fellow Christian and he felt the need to reinforce the fact that I was supposed to put on my own oxygen mask first before I rushed around to help others. I still find it interesting to this day that he chose to share this bit of advice with me. Whatever he was observing about my behavior at work, he obviously felt the need to step in and give me a little fatherly advice. I must admit that it was good advice and I took it in the way that it was intended.

I learned from him that it is perfectly okay to first take care of my own needs in certain instances in order to better see to others and their needs. Not everything said or read is so black and white. This gentleman took the time to educate me because he felt it was necessary to do so. For whatever reason, he thought I was risking my own health in order to serve others. He stepped outside of his comfort zone to explain this concept to me. I thanked him for steering me in the right direction. By using this analogy, I figuratively learned to first put on my own oxygen mask in life in order to make sure I was there for the long haul. In doing so, I could better serve others according to God's Plan and not my own.

At times, it is not only appropriate but very necessary to put our needs ahead of others to ensure that we can actually serve God in the way that we were meant to serve. This man served me that day and I have learned to serve others in much the same way. If I don't have my oxygen mask on, I'm not going to last very long and I won't be of any use at all.

"The highest reward for a person's toil is not what he gets for it, but what he becomes by it." ~ John Ruskin

Personal Reflections:

1. Do you agree with the advice given to me by the gentleman in this story?
2. If so, do you take the necessary precautions to protect yourself so that you will have the staying power to stand the test of time?
3. If not, do you see yourself as the kind of person that must always come last? If so, why?
4. For those of you who think that you should come last in order to serve God, are you certain this is God's

will for you? At times, it is very difficult to discern the difference between our will and the image we want to project and what God's will actually is for us. This effort requires much prayer, discernment, and open-mindedness.

7 ~ Dysfunctional Mother/Daughter Relationships

"Within our dreams and aspirations we find our opportunities." ~ Sue Atchley Ebaugh

Over the Christmas Season, I had the opportunity to enjoy a few movies. For several days, both my husband and I were struggling with the flu and colds. It was a great opportunity to find some enjoyment during the recuperating period by watching movies on TV. My husband went to bed earlier than usual one evening because he was feeling so under the weather. While I was channel hopping I came across a movie that was already in progress. It was a simple, little movie that would appeal to all age groups but probably more to children than to adults.

It was the story about two mothers who were extremely different. One was a teacher who was very concerned about the education of her teenage daughter. Her main desire was to see her daughter excel academically and to get accepted into Harvard. The other mother was an ice skating coach. She, on the other hand, wanted her daughter to excel at ice skating and perhaps qualify for the Olympics. As you have probably already guessed, it was as if each of these mothers had given birth to the wrong daughter. The daughter with the academic mother was a gifted skater and it was her dream to be an Olympic champion. The daughter of the ice skating coach wasn't at all interested in following in her mother's footsteps. She wanted to excel academically.

Both mothers refused to look at what their daughters aspired to be and only looked at what they wanted for their daughters. They both thought that they knew best and were extremely adamant about it. The academic mother went so far as to refuse to even go watch her daughter skate. She was totally unaware of how gifted her daughter was in this area. She was very closed-minded. In essence, both these mothers were living vicariously through their daughters. They actually wanted their daughters to succeed where they had failed. They were both so controlling in trying to accomplish their own end goals.

How many of us are just like that? We have our own agenda and we look at what we want without giving any thought to what anyone else wants.

It doesn't necessarily have to be in a dysfunctional mother/daughter relationship. This lack of communication and unattractive power struggle can be found in any relationship. Balance…equality…mutual respect. These may appear to be lofty goals but with honesty, desire, and hard work, they are definitely attainable and well worth the effort.

"You will become as small as your controlling desire, as great as your dominant aspiration." ~ *James Allen*

Personal Reflections:

1. Are we really looking at the people in our lives from their point of view? This is no easy task. What do you think?
2. Do you feel that you must suppress whom you really are in order to stay in a relationship or do you feel the need to be in charge because you are insecure or threatened by those around you?
3. If things don't go your way, do you try to accept the situation in a mature way or do you lash out?

8 ~ Storage Bins

"We do not remember days, we remember moments."
~ Pavese, Cesar

Life is like a closet full of clothes. It's very difficult to know what you want to give away, donate, or discard. It's even harder to discard some of those items that have been given to you as gifts or those that have sentimental value. Some of these items may have little or no monetary worth but they fill our drawers and our storage bins. I have many such items that I cannot part with because they mean so much to me.

If I keep these items, will they have any special meaning to my children or my grandchildren? The last birthday card signed "with love" by my mother-in-law before she died over twenty years ago, the ripped sheet of paper from an old prayer-book with my father's signature so proudly written on it, the scribbled notes that my granddaughter left in the bathroom cupboard, the popcorn pictures and artwork from my other grandchildren, and the albums of numerous pictures that my husband has so conscientiously organized…who will want these treasures that I have saved?

When I was seventeen years old, my then boyfriend was chosen to go on a school trip to Vancouver, BC. On his return, he gave me a beautiful sweater. That was almost fifty years ago. That boyfriend became my husband, my friend, my lover, my confidant. Who will want that "holey" not "holy" sweater I have so carefully wrapped and stored in some box in my basement? Our children are going to have a huge laugh on us one day as they sort through our belongings and discover how sentimental we are.

To continue in this vein, when I was a very young girl my father gave me a blunt-ended little hammer. One morning as I was walking with my girlfriends, we started to discuss how sentimental we've all become as we age. We've discovered that keepsakes actually matter much more to us now than they did in our youth.

One friend was explaining this fact by sharing a story with us. She said she went through a lot of work and effort to make small quilts that she gave as presents to her children and grandchildren. After they were used for their initial purpose and as the years went by, they were eventually used in some other constructive way. The other way she noticed was that they ended up at the bottom of the dog kennel. By the pained expression on her face, it seemed to me that she would have preferred that her children were more sentimental. It was also apparent to me that she hoped they would cherish these homemade quilts in much the same way that they were created...with love. Perhaps in her children's opinion they were cherished because they did indeed love their dogs.

I then took this opportunity to share my story about my handy little hammer with my friends. It goes like this. Many years ago when I was a preschooler and several times thereafter, I used to work in the garage with my Dad. He was a self-taught carpenter as well as a general handy man. I loved to spend time with him in whatever way possible. During one of these special times, he gave me a small hammer to call my own. Over the years, I didn't think too much about that hammer but when I got married over forty-five years ago and left home, my Dad gave it to me.

A couple of months ago, one of my granddaughters phoned and asked if she could spend the day with us. I quickly agreed to this request. Her dad was on his way out and he promptly dropped her off at our house. Grandpa was busy hanging pictures using my cherished little hammer so I asked our granddaughter to hand the hammer to grandpa when he needed it. I then explained to my six-year-old granddaughter that I used this very hammer when I was about her age. She looked at me with that quizzical look of hers and asked "really". I'm sure she wondered if I was ever really that young.

I proceeded to tell her how precious this hammer was to me because it was a gift from my father. I further added that one day I would love to give it to her but I wanted to wait until she could realize the importance of it. I definitely want to pass my hammer along. Even as simple and as old as this gift may be, I want her to keep it and do the same. Now isn't that silly? Well not "really", at least not to me. My hammer signifies a lovely memory and a cherished part of my life. The words that I write have much the same meaning. My words are my hammer. It's why I write. I want my words to be passed along down the line to all who are willing to read them. I have a message. My message means an awful lot to me. In my early thirties I dreamed of writing a book to share my message. After twenty-five years of dreaming, I finally got started and haven't stopped since.

"You are never too old to set another goal or dream a new dream." ~ C.S. Lewis

Personal Reflections:

1. Do you have a message or any special mementoes that you would like to keep in your family?

2. Do you consider yourself to be a sentimental person?
3. Have you become more sentimental with age?
4. Does anyone else share in your sentimental pleasure of simple things?
5. Do you struggle with parting with these items? If so, in my opinion, that's a good thing. Trust me, you are not alone.

9 ~ Taking Notice

"Life is either a daring adventure or nothing." ~ *Helen Keller*

Once and awhile I am inspired to veer off in another direction. I see this as a chance to either lighten up or to inject a little variety into my stories by looking at things from a different angle. As you've probably already gathered, I am a thinker. When I published my first book, my editor sent me a little message. She suggested that I write more and think less. I tried my best to comply. It was not an easy request for me. I have to admit that I do a lot of meditating especially in the wee hours of the morning. I also do my fair share of reflecting and analyzing life and the challenges it poses. Oftentimes, I also find great pleasure and entertainment in people watching or observing simple human behavior. One of these occasions has prompted me to ask the following questions.

When people take group pictures and show you the results, whose face do you look for when viewing the developed product? When there is some kind of contest or game that you have subscribed to and a list of winners is provided, who do you look for in the slate of names? When you make a subtle change with your appearance or lifestyle do you expect people to notice? When you speak, do you expect people to listen?

All these questions…where could I possibly be going with this? Well, if you are anything like me, these questions were quite simple to answer. I am no different than any one of you. When I know I'm in a photo, I zoom into the picture of me to see how I look. When winners or names are announced or posted, I immediately look to see where I stand. When I change my appearance or wear something new, I hope somebody will notice and perhaps make a comment or compliment me on the change. I definitely appreciate when my friends and family listen to what I have to say and show an interest in the topic or news that I am sharing with them.

After admitting this not only to myself but to my readers as well, I then proceed to go one step further. I frequently ask myself if I do the same for others in much the same way that I hope or expect them to do for me. I feel it is necessary to remind myself that I can't ask a desired behavior from others if I am not prepared to deliver it myself. Plain and simple, in order to look at and listen to others more effectively, we must make a conscious decision to offer this same consideration.

Therefore, I can merely ask one more question. Are you taking the time to really notice someone or something about another person other than focusing on yourself? If you are, this is what relationship building is all about.

The title of this little chapter **Taking Notice** reminds me of an incident that took place in a social function some time ago. I am what most people would consider to be the average Joe. I am very down to earth and I pretty well blend in wherever I go. I am not the kind of person that stands out and for all intents and purposes, I am not comfortable with being the center of attention. In a very small group of four to six people, I can be seen as the life of the party but in a larger group I seem to fade away. In other words, I'm far more an introvert than an extrovert.

Many years ago I attended a large staff Christmas party with my husband. Actually it was his staff party and I knew very few people which I admit, contributed to my awkwardness in this type of situation. The wife of one of my husband's co-workers came up to me later on in the evening and made a comment to me that I have never forgotten.

She said, *"You are the type of person that no one would ever notice when they first walked into a room. However, if they took the time to take a second look, they would never forget you".*

I hardly knew this woman, yet her words had a profound effect on me. At first blush, as already mentioned, I'm an average looking person. Also, as I said before, I really don't stand out in any way, shape or form. I seldom draw attention to myself by anything I say, do, or wear in these types of situations. In fact, I will usually go out of my way to avoid the limelight in these large group settings.

What this woman said to me was a two-sided comment. I sensed that she meant it as a compliment and chose to see the bright side and learn from her words. How many people appear to be just like the average Joe? If or when we take the time to have a second look and draw them out, we may be very pleasantly surprised by what we discover.

Some people are very comfortable with being in the center of things and have no trouble drawing attention to themselves. In fact, it is very natural for them to do so. For those that aren't nearly as comfortable, it's a great idea for us to take the time to have a second look and see what we might have missed the first time around.

I'm grateful to that woman who managed to teach me this very simple yet valuable lesson. I have been taking a second look at the people around me ever since. It has paid off big time and I have discovered many diamonds in the rough.

"Give the world the best that you have, and the best will come back to you." ~ Madeline Bridges"

Personal Reflections:

1. Do you like being the center of attention?
2. Would you consider yourself to be an introvert or an extrovert?
3. Do you take the time to truly notice those around you and give them more than a passing glance?
4. Do you agree that we might miss some very meaningful friendships by not taking a second look?

10 ~ The Three Faces of Eve

"Never mistake knowledge for wisdom. One helps you make a living; the other helps you make a life." ~ Sandra Carey

Over fifteen years ago, due to a job change by my husband, we decided to move to a small town. It had a population of about 900 people and was situated about a two-hour drive from the large city which had been our home for most of our lives. At this time, our three daughters were not yet married, although one was already on her own. The other two, our nineteen year old twins, were full-time university students still living at home. I was working full-time at a major financial institution. From my point of view, this was what I considered to be a major lifestyle change. We found an apartment for the girls, sold our house, quit our jobs, and moved to this quaint little town. We lived there for six years.

On looking back, I don't know how we did it. It had a huge impact on all of us. Our girls found their independence after the usual trials and tribulations. My husband settled into his job and I did the best I could to fill the void in my life. This was the first time in several years that I didn't work outside the home. I became involved in a variety of volunteer projects in order to amuse myself and fill my now long days.

One of the things I decided to do, was to take a few painting classes. I did not have an artistic bone in my body up to this point and I had no idea what to expect. I bought my supplies and proceeded to try to learn how to be an artist. I didn't go to many classes, but I still persisted in painting on my own. During the six-year period in this small town, I painted numerous pictures. Once we moved back to the big city just over fifteen years ago, I never painted again.

When living in Pine Falls, my husband used to tease me and say that I was one of the most prolific painters he had ever seen. During this six-year period, I probably painted thirty-five pictures. I never sold one painting, although, a few people were gracious enough to accept the odd gift. Most paintings were "the pits" even from my own standards but there are a few that I cherish. Three of them remain very special to me even to this day and I have them hanging in our home.

This first painting is picture of a young girl about the age of eight years old. She is very sad and she symbolizes a "sorrowful child". The second picture is also of a young girl. She is probably in her early teens and of Amish descent. From the outside, you can see that there is no physical relationship between the two girls. I refer to this girl as a "shy youth". The third painting is that of an older native woman and once again appears to bear no relationship to the other two paintings. I call this painting a "wiser older woman". She represents what I consider myself to be similar to today as I am an older woman compared to the first two young girls. It has taken many years and many personal trials and tribulations to arrive at this point in my life.

    I call these combined portraits, "The Three Faces of Eve" because they show the distinct facets and faces of my own personality and the stages I have gone through to become who I am today. I am not alone. Each of us has many different facets to our personalities. These three distinct faces demonstrate my own personal growth. They are actually an x-ray view of myself. I have used a unique and creative way to paint a self-portrait. I have chosen to paint myself from the inside out to demonstrate my maturation process.

    We all have hidden talents. It took me a long time to realize what some of mine might be. True growth is discovering whom we really are and having both the courage and the freedom to express it.

    This experience has been very liberating for me and one I have learned to truly appreciate.

"History has demonstrated that the most notable winners usually encountered heartbreaking obstacles before they triumphed." ~ B.C. Forbes

Personal Reflections:

1. Have you had a good look at yourself lately?
2. Are you tapping into your creative abilities?
3. What does your x-ray (innermost self) look like? Our outside image or persona may be very different from our x-ray view.
4. Are you being true to yourself or do you hide behind a false image or facade?
5. Have you dared to remove your mask and truly be who you were meant to be?

11 ~ Spit It Out

"Love is everything. It is the key to life, and its influences are those that move the world." ~ Ralph Waldo Trine

My husband of over forty-five years is a pretty silent man. I married my high school sweetheart. No, we weren't the prom king and queen. As a matter of fact, he actually got chosen and I didn't. He was so gallant that he refused to accept this honor because he didn't want someone else by his side to share in this momentous teenage moment.

It's seems like a lifetime ago that we were playing the dating game in our eleventh grade classroom. My then boyfriend grabbed my attention right at the onset. Boy…he was one quiet guy and I sure made up for his silence when we were together.

Not too long ago, I had the sneaking suspicion that I said something to offend him. I wasn't a hundred percent sure because we were just heading off to bed after a late night with friends, but come morning there was no doubt about it.

By now you are probably asking yourself "how does a silent man tell you that you have offended him?" Body language, that's how!

When "Silent Sam" woke up at his usual time, I had been up and at it for about three hours. He got his usual cup of coffee and sat in his rocking chair across from me. That's not out of the ordinary. He gets up, gets his coffee, sits in silence and waits for me to say something to start our day.

Something was subtlety different this morning and a less experienced eye might have missed it. He did all the above mentioned things but in addition to these, he crossed his arms and then I knew for sure that I had offended him. He seldom crosses his arms first thing in the morning.

I knew he had "a burr in his saddle" and I suggested he "spit it out" so that we could get on with our day. That's exactly what he did after a little prodding from me. We then discussed what was bothering him and he got it off his chest. I've learned that it's best not to let things fester. It's far better to "spit it out" and then get on with life. Life's much too short to harbor resentment. Don't you think that it's much better to clear the air and move on?

Now, over forty-five years later, he is a little more talkative and I am a lot less than I was in our youth. Although, I still can outdo my husband, I have nowhere near as much to say these days. I find that we have long moments of silence in our home and it's not one bit awkward. We've discovered that we can still be in each other's company and provide a sense of comfort with silence. I like it and so does he. The pressure to fill the silence has been removed a long time ago as we embrace each other in this wonderful and pleasant way.

Yes…silence is okay too. In fact, in most instances I have come to cherish it and my husband is okay with it too. I may not have been chosen to be prom queen but my husband has done his best to treat me like royalty whenever possible. He can still be gallant these days too.

"Harmony is one phase of the great law whose spiritual expression is love." ~ James Allen

"A true friend is one who is concerned about what we are becoming, who sees beyond the present relationship, and who cares deeply about us as a whole person." ~ Gloria Gaither

Personal Reflections:

1. When a problem arises in any of your relationships, do you address it as soon as possible?
2. Do you agree that this is the wisest course of action?
3. Have you noticed that if you don't, the problem can morph into an even bigger one?

4. Do you manage to keep calm when facing a problematic situation or do you let anger get the best of you?
5. Do you ever go to bed angry or do you try your best to get over unpleasant situations so that they don't affect your emotional wellbeing?

12 ~ On Being Tested ~ Fred Ayotte

Now a few words of wisdom from my husband...

Many times in life we are tested by people in order to see if they can get a reaction out of us. We have all met someone who makes a comment or behaves in a way that is out of the norm. They are waiting to see how we will respond. If we are smart enough to realize what they are doing, we can really have fun by responding in a totally different way than they might expect. It is as if we've turned the table around and now their reaction to our unexpected response is sometimes worth the price. Two people can play the same game, don't you think?

This theory often holds true when teenagers interact with parents. I have been blessed with three beautiful daughters. When my oldest daughter was growing up everything was new to me as a parent. So as a father, I may have over reacted to certain behaviors based on my lack of experience. However, when my twins came along, I had learned to take things in better stride. One of my twin daughters who is now a beautiful, kind, and sensitive woman, went through a rebellious stage in her teens.

She had long beautiful hair which enhanced her good looks. I remember one day she came home from school and announced to her mother and me that she was shaving her head. She was about fifteen years old at the time and she wanted to make a statement...true beauty is on the inside of a person and she wanted to be regarded as a beautiful person. In other words, she had every desire for people to look at her kind and compassionate personality. My wife was very upset. I told her not to worry because the act of our daughter shaving her head was far better than a lot of other things that she could possibly be doing.

I remember vividly the night she came home with her hair all cut off. My wife had gone to bed and I was sitting in the living room. I think my daughter expected me to react to the bald look. All I did was go up to her, rub her head and say "hmmm fuzzy" and walk away. I don't know what reaction she expected to get from me but none was given other than this warm gesture. It wasn't too long after that, her hair grew back and we went on to the next issue.

Please note: The questions I am about to ask are created by me, not my husband.

Personal Reflections:

1. If there is one thing I learned from my husband in the previous situation...it is to not sweat the small stuff. Do you do just that?
2. Do you work yourself up over trivial things only to realize later on that it was no big deal?
3. Do you know how to put things into perspective in order to be more reasonable and less emotional when a problematic situation arises?

13 ~ Objections Anyone...

"Life is either a daring adventure or nothing. To keep our faces toward change and behave like free spirits in the presence of fate...is strength undefeatable." ~ *Helen Keller*

When I was graduating from high school, it seemed that there weren't many career choices for me. I'm not so sure if it was the fact that I was a female or if it had to do more with my financial situation or merely just plain lack of opportunity. Perhaps, it was a combination of all three.

In my nuclear family, it was far more the exception to get a university degree than it was the rule. Out of six children, only two of us attended university. I am sure the rest of my siblings would have enjoyed attaining a higher education as it certainly wasn't their lack of intelligence that kept them away…only a lack of opportunity and more than likely a lack of financial resources. A university degree was not easy to attain especially in my situation. I only managed to receive my degree on a part-time basis after I got married and while raising my young family.

Upon graduating from high school, it seemed that the majority of females, although not all, chose some kind of secretarial work, teaching, or nursing career. I was no different. A one year teacher certification program was being offered for free due to the shortage of teachers in our province. I jumped at the chance. I then proceeded to further educate myself at my own financial expense.

When I look at my high school year book, under my picture is the caption, Dolores "wants to be a lawyer...objections anyone?" As I recall that comment, I smile to myself. Today, I know for certain I am a teacher but I must admit, there is still something inside of me that is every bit the lawyer. I don't mean when it comes to matters of law, as much as the desire to "defend" a person who is being slandered or to "defend" a worthy cause. I figure we can have all kinds of "callings" without an official designation. What do you think? I am sure that I am not the only one that chose a different career option due to circumstance whether personal or financial. Perhaps like me, circumstances prevented you from fulfilling your initial dream or aspiration but maybe you've figured out how to feel rewarded nonetheless.

"The golden opportunity you are seeking is in yourself. It is not in your environment; it is not in luck or chance, or the help of others; it is in yourself alone." ~ *Orison Swett Marden*

Personal Reflections:

1. If you have a calling that is yet to be realized, what is it?
2. Is there still a chance that you might have another career or do you consider it to be too late?
3. If you were unable to follow your heart for whatever reason in your younger years, have you found a creative way to incorporate your initial career aspiration into your life in order to feel more fulfilled?

14 ~ The Weather Channel ~ On a Lighter Note

A little humor can go a long way...

Sometimes in life I feel like I am a cross between Erma Bombeck with her wry sense of humor and Phyllis Diller and her silliness about her husband, Fang. To quote Phyllis, she states that "his fine hour lasted about a minute and a half." I sincerely hope that some of you know who these two admirable women are even though Erma has now left her legacy with us and Phyllis is still hanging in there. I love both these women because they have such delightful senses of humor and they have succeeded in making a lot of people laugh over the years.

How great is that when you can bring a smile to someone's face, or light up their eyes with mirth, or get a burst of laughter that seems to come from the tips of their toes? Oh...to bring such pleasure and joy to other human beings. What a wonderful goal to strive for and to emulate. My desire to be similar to either of these two well-known women is quite the aspiration.

When a couple retires, they get a good taste at developing the kind of sense of humor it truly takes to sustain a long time marriage and ride off into the sunset together. During these retirement years, you have the opportunity to discover what your marriage vows are all about and what it really means to say "I do". When there is no one else to look at, you have plenty of time to have a better look at your lifelong partner. Some don't make it after almost a life time together. Just take a look at Al Gore and his wife Tipper. After forty years of marriage they bid each other adieu, even after that big smooch we observed on national television just a few short years ago.

One of the initial signs of being true retirees is when you have the Weather Channel on TV tuned in for several hours during the day. Your love is tested when you ask your husband what kind of weather to expect and he looks at you, points to his forehead and asks, "Do you see a weathervane on my forehead?" I cannot tell you how many times I've had that response when I ask my husband what it is like outside before I dress for our daily walk. In other words, do I need a jacket or don't I?

Hey, it could be worse. I could have to look at the Weather Channel myself. I much prefer to delegate this small task to my husband instead. You just can't help but love this guy. He's a real stand-up kind of fellow but sometimes I think he should be a sit–down-comedian as he shoots out his humorous commentary from his rocking chair in the den. Perhaps he is trying to emulate Jack Benny. He never ceases to amaze me with his one liners. He probably wouldn't mind using one of Jack's famous quotes right about now. Jack has been known to say, *"My wife Mary and I have been married forty-seven years, and not once have we had an argument serious enough to consider divorce…murder, yes…divorce, never."*

My husband really does watch the Weather Channel but he insists he's listening to the music. What do you think?

Here's another peek at the life of a longtime married couple just to give a heads up of what you have to look forward to if you haven't been married as long we have. A few years ago, my husband had double cataract surgery. His vision could no longer be corrected adequately enough with eyeglasses so it was recommended that he get new lenses. My husband has worn thick glasses ever since he was a young boy. As a result of the surgery, he ended up with extremely good distant vision. He now has 20/20 vision when seeing far away.

On the way home from the eye doctor after removal of the first patch, I could have sworn he was winking at me. He kept opening and closing his eye because he couldn't believe the difference in his vision. The colors were so bright. He repeatedly placed his hand on-and-off his good eye in his state of disbelief at what he could now see. Good thing I was driving, which is unusual in itself, but his now improved vision was equally unusual and he was extremely impressed with the results.

After his second eye surgery, he got his eyes retested and the prescription he received was for glasses that would accommodate his now, no-so-good "near" vision, a common side effect of cataract surgery. However, there was no way that this man was going to wear glasses…not after wearing them almost his entire life. He felt certain that he didn't need to wear glasses anymore. He then decided he could make do with glasses from the dollar store in order to read instead of getting the prescription that the eye doctor recommended.

Well, let me tell you, if we don't have ten pairs of glasses lying all around the house, we don't have one. They are on or in every nook and cranny you can imagine. Every time I talk to my husband when he's reading the newspaper, he peers over the top of his glasses at me. He needs glasses to read but to not see me across the room. I must admit, he looks quite professorial. I think God played a little trick on me. Now I am an older woman and my husband can see me even better than he did in his youth. Does that sound fair to you? Good thing he has some tact.

Personal Reflections:
1. Do you use humor in your life as often as possible?
2. Are you in a long term relationship? If so, can you relate to the need for a sense of humor?
3. Do you ever take a moment to really laugh with your partner or anyone else for that matter?

15 ~ Early Bird ~ More on a Lighter Note

"A bird doesn't sing because it has an answer, it sings because it has a song." ~ Maya Angelou

Is it true? Does the early bird really catch the worm? Every morning, it's the very same thing. No matter what time I go to bed at night, my internal clock wakes me up at about 5:00 am. In a sense, I should be annoyed and grumpy because a part of me would like to sleep in like other non-morning people. The other part of me loves this alone time.

I cannot tell you how productive I am first thing in the morning. I have anywhere between two to three hours before my husband saunters into the den with his morning cup of coffee. I kind of feel sorry for him because after several hours of quiet, albeit productive time, I am ready to talk to someone.

He's the only someone around and I'm sure, at times, he would like to press my off button this early in the morning. Trust me, it is already late from my frame of reference and I am eager to get started on the rest of my day.

I must admit that I have to back off just a little so that my husband can have a few moments of relaxation to enjoy his cup of coffee and newspaper first thing in the morning. He has the same right to do so even if it is almost three hours later than me. Hey, different personalities…it's what keeps us challenged as we learn to respect each other's differences.

I have the sneaking suspicion that early birds can get on some people's nerves now and then. I'm sure I rub my husband the wrong way occasionally. I realize that I can get on his only nerve with my morning chatter, but what the heck! We're two older birds in this empty nest of ours and we can enjoy life the way we see fit. We know how to work it out.

Yes…I'm a morning person. There's no getting around that fact. Most mornings I'm up before the crack of dawn, even before the sun pops up.

I can hardly ever remember getting up on the wrong side of the bed. Morning people are an odd bunch. Usually we can hardly wait to start the day and I'm no exception. I vividly recall one such memory that took place many years ago on the way to work with my husband. As I was humming along to a song, he suggested that if I was going to "chirp" all the way to work at 7:00 in the morning, I might have to consider taking a bus. Ouch!

Yes…my husband is the exact opposite. At times, he gives new meaning to the term grumpy first thing in the morning. As the day progresses, his face eventually lights up and so does his mood. By evening I can hardly recognize his sunny nature as my day starts to wind down. When they say that opposites attract, we certainly prove it in this area of our marriage.

My day coach turns back into a pumpkin long before midnight and certainly long before the big guy, as I lovingly refer to him, hits the sack.

My dad used to say, "It takes all kinds to make the world go around". How true. We're comparable to eggs. I'm sunny side up and my husband is scrambled. I'm relieved to say that he is definitely not hard-boiled. I like it that way. It provides for variety in our lives as it challenges us to learn how to respect each other's differences. It has been said that "variety is the spice of life". I know this to be true and I have a sneaking suspicion you do too.

"Personal relationships are the fertile soil from which all advancement, all success, all achievement in real life grows." ~ Ben Stein

Personal Reflections:

1. Are you an early bird or a late riser?
2. Who do you think is easier to live with or to be?

3. Do you adjust your schedule to accommodate your partner or is it the other way around?
4. If you both have the same time schedule, do you ever crave alone time at either the beginning or end of the day?

16 ~ Sadness

Sometimes, I also feel an overwhelming sense of sadness. My initial reaction is to try to push it away. I find it difficult to dwell in this experience. I then realize that if I sit in this moment and think through what is causing the sadness, I learn to make more sense of it.

Perhaps I have every reason to be sad upon hearing that my good friend has been diagnosed with cancer or that someone I love is going through a difficult time. It is okay for me to accept and embrace this sadness as I work through the pain of what others are experiencing. It is not necessary for me to push it away. It is only necessary for me to pray for these people and know that the moment will pass.

Sadly to say, it may take a long time for their moment to pass, so the least I can do is share in their suffering by not only being sad for them but by praying for them as well.

Personal Reflections:
1. Do you ever feel sad?
2. If so, why? Just know, it's okay to feel all of our emotions.

17 ~ The Art of Playing Cards ~ Fred Ayotte ~ More on a Lighter Note

Written by my husband…

"I love the winning, I can take the losing, but most of all I love to play the game. " ~ Boris Becker

I grew up in a household where card playing was a family tradition. From an early age, I learned how to play children's games such as War, Go Fish, and Old Maid. As I grew older, my parents taught me how to play Hearts, Barouche, Cribbage, and more advanced card games. Therefore, as my daughters were growing up, carrying on this long time family tradition of playing cards came naturally.

When they were very young, one of their favorite games was Go Fish. We would literally play for hours. As much as I loved playing this game with them, I would get quite tired after a while especially after a long day at work. However, they never wanted to quit.

As you know, the game of Go Fish is about the matching of cards. You start by asking the other player if they have a certain card. If the answer is yes, they must give it to you. If not, then you just pick one from the deck. After hours of playing, if my young daughters didn't have the card I asked for, I eventually would pick one from the deck. I then put it in my matched cards pile whether they were a pair or not. Soon afterwards, the game would end. Nobody could figure out why they ended up with unmatched cards in their hands. I know some of you may call this cheating...I called it relief. It was time for the game to finally be over and for them to go to bed so that I could have a bit of an evening with my wife.

It wasn't until many years later that my daughters put two-and-two together and figured out what I had been up to so many years earlier. We all had a good laugh about it. What I didn't realize was that my oldest granddaughter Abby, who was about five at the time, was listening. She is now eighteen.

A few years later during one of our many visits to spend time with our eldest daughter and her family, Abby wanted us to play cards with her and her younger sister. They wanted to play Go Fish to be exact. Abby who was then eight years old was organizing the seating. She was telling her mother and grandmother where to sit as well as her younger sister Becca who was five. Becca is now fifteen. After Abby got everyone seated to her satisfaction, she looked right at me in a very serious demeanor and said "Grandpa, you sit beside me. I want to keep my eye on you because I hear you cheat at Go Fish". My wife and daughter just burst out laughing.

Alas, my reputation had caught up to me after all these years. Everyone had a good laugh and no one has let me forget it since.

Little ears…they hear everything! Are you setting a good example for your children and grandchildren?

18 ~ The Persistence of the Spirit
~ Andrea Ayotte Cockerill

Written by my daughter...

"What lies behind us and what lies before us are tiny matters compared to what lies within us." ~ Oliver Wendell Holmes

If you have ever been around children, you know how persistent they can be when they want your attention. All of my children let me know in their own way if they feel like they are not getting their fair share of my time. Today it was my oldest daughter who told me loud and clear that her well for my attention was running low.

After filling my daughter's desire for personal attention, I started thinking about how persistent our spirit can be when we are ignoring its guidance and passions. I have on many occasions put my spirit last on the list because I am comforted with the fact that my spirit is going nowhere. No matter how long I ignore it...it is like a patient and trusted friend, waiting for my next phone call.

Our relationship with our spirit is like any other relationship that we honor in our lives. It needs our time in order for an intimate bond to be built. It is the difference between talking to one friend every few months and talking to another friend every few days. You may cherish both friends but it is the friend whom you talk to more often that is going to know the more intimate details of your daily life. This same principle applies to our spirit. If we form an intimate relationship with our spirit, we will be better able to understand and intuitively follow its subtle guidance system.

Your spirit promises you that it will never reject you. It is persistent but patient, and its sole goal is to lead you to the Divine. Forming a relationship with your spirit needs to be a conscious decision on a daily basis, but the rewards span a life time.

Namaste ~ I see the Divine in you which is also in me.

"Continuous effort is the key to unlocking our potential." ~ *Black Elk, Native American*

"The spirit, the will to win, and the will to excel are the things that endure." ~ *Vince Lombardi*

19 ~ Leadership

"Real leaders are ordinary people with extraordinary determination." ~ Source Unknown

I have a dear friend in my life that I have known since I was six years old. We started off in first grade together. This particular friend is a born leader. Ever since I can remember when it came to electing class presidents, she was the one chosen. She has incredible leadership skills and organizational qualities. This friend has held several jobs and each and every one of them has always been in management. If she doesn't start off with the position, she inevitably ends up with it. If there is anyone who knows how to get a job done, it is her.

Not all people are so lucky that their personalities are so distinctive or apparent. I think the reverse of being a true leader also applies to the characteristics of being a true follower. Both personalities stand out and can more often-than-not be clearly identified. At times; however, being seen as a follower doesn't necessarily endear you to others or even to yourself. Born leaders or take charge people don't always understand or have compassion for those who need to be given more direction and encouragement along the way.

When we don't address our personality type, we could possibly become aggravated when we lose patience with others in our effort to provide guidance.

I also know that there is a grey zone when it comes to these two very different personalities. Nothing is ever that cut and dry in life. I can very much say that I have traits that fall into both zones. You may very well be the same as I think this personality description is far more common than the other two. Some people may even classify the combination of the two opposite personalities as passive-aggressive types. I am not so sure that I agree with this evaluation but it certainly is a popular term these days. However, I do think that by engaging in a real honest self-evaluation, we can decide which category we fall into. In doing so, we can learn to better handle some of the changes we might want to make in our lives. Thus we can become more responsible and accountable for our own happiness.

"In the last analysis, the individual person is responsible for living his own life and for 'finding himself'. If he insists in shifting his responsibility to somebody else, he fails to find out the meaning of his own existence." ~ **Thomas Merton**

As previously stated, there is absolutely nothing wrong with either personality. It all boils down to self-acceptance and mutual respect for each other. We aren't all made from the same mold. Life would be very boring if we were. Therefore, the ultimate goal is to learn to appreciate ourselves for whom we are and to change the things about ourselves that are changeable. It is extremely difficult to alter an innate part of our basic being. We can't expect others to do things our way either. We need all types of personalities to effectively make this world of ours go around.

If you are a follower, the key is to follow the right people. If you are a leader, the key is to lead others in an admirable direction. There is a huge difference between leading people and trying to control or bossing them. The difference is as clear as night and day. If you fall somewhere in between the distinct personalities of a leader or follower, use your God-given talents in both areas as wisely as possible. The best way to deal with all personality types is to realize our own individual make-up, to evaluate what we have to offer in any given situation, and to work toward achieving a common goal for the greater good. We can all achieve our goals if we learn to better work together. Each personality has its inherent advantages and disadvantages. We need each other in order to have a more balanced world. I always try to remind myself that no one can accomplish a whole heck of a lot on their own. Leaders need followers in order to accomplish their desired goal. Followers also need great leaders to emulate in helping to get the job done. Those people that have a balance between the two have their work cut out for them. They must discern when to be a pilot or when to be a passenger. It takes great skill to effectively and efficiently learn when to step in to get the job done or to butt out when it is being done the right way.

"There is no higher service than human service. To work for the common good is the greatest creed." ~ *Albert Schweitzer*

Personal Reflections:

1. Okay…now for a little truth serum. What personality category best suits you? Are you a born leader, a follower, or a combination of the two?
2. If so, do you like yourself in this role? If not, why?
3. To born leaders…when others need too much guidance from you do you get frustrated with them? In other words, do you end up resenting them at times?
4. To born followers…when people try to guide you more than you would like, do you get frustrated with

them? Do you eventually resent them and see them as trying to take control of your life?

5. To those with both capabilities...do you know when to use your leadership qualities and when not to?

20 ~ A New Word to Make You Smile

I heard a new word not so long ago on TV for the very first time. I honestly don't think it's a real word or that you could find it in any dictionary but I really like the sound of it. The word is "smize". Actually it is probably spelled "sm-eyes". I'm not quite sure of the correct spelling but it is actually irrelevant to what I am about to share with you. I merely want to ask if you've ever heard this word before and do you know what it means?

Before I tell you what this TV host said it means, I want to ask you another question. Have you ever heard the expression that the "eyes are the window to the soul"? I love this saying because when I look into people's eyes, I see their spirit. Sometimes, I see kindness, joy, sadness, anger, and so on. I think the eyes really do give away our innermost feelings if we let them. The expression reflected in our eyes can really make us feel quite vulnerable. I think our eyes are our most precious feature and clearly demonstrate our inner beauty if that is what lies there. In fact, I think the eyes are the most expressive physical feature we have and the one I certainly value the most.

Okay, so now back to the meaning of this so-called new word. I gave you a bit of a clue to its meaning when I clarified the spelling. "Sm-eyes" means to "smile with your eyes". I like the meaning of this new word. To me, when our whole face lights up when we smile, is what true "sm-eyesing" is really all about. Several times in my life, I have heard the expression, he or she smiled in such a way but the smile never quite reached their eyes. Does that make sense to you? Have you ever smiled as you look into a mirror? Hey, give it a try. You've got nothing to lose. Have a good look and see what other people see when you smile at them. In other words…do you sm-eyes? The answer to this question is far more important than anyone of us might fully realize.

When I was extrapolating on the meaning of this new word with one of my friends Charles Betts as he shared with me on my blog site. *"I think the word "sm-eyes"…smiling with our eyes and its concept are a beneficial principle to apply to our daily routines. The eyes are for sure a window to the soul. I have known some people in life who have, due to rough circumstances in life, drawn the shades over the windows and refuse to let people see in. From my perspective it appears they feel that if no-one sees in then they are safe. They feel that any intruders are there only to take things from their soul which they do not want to give away or share.*

Their world becomes smaller and tighter and they eventually dry up inside.

When my two daughters were in their formative years and would come home from school, having been hurt or disappointed by their friends, they would express a desire to have nothing to do with that friend. I would say: If you continue to cut off your friends when they hurt you, eventually you will end up in a small circle by yourself". I wanted them to learn that pain will come but we must overcome the pain with love and forgiveness. Love will never dry up as long as we let it flow. Only when we dam it up inside does it dry up.

To get back to the word "sm-eyes", yes...we do benefit when we learn to let our eyes express the beauty of our souls. If someone abuses that beauty then they have some issues in their own soul. They need our friendship and prayers. As does God deal with us, we can be blessed when we love because it is in us, not because someone deserves it. In this way we are in control of our own happiness, not those we deal with. So it is that we "sm-eyes" all those we contact. Both they and we are blessed."

Personal Reflections:

1. This personal reflection is going to be plain and simple. Do you "sm-eyes" and if not, why not?

2. Are you trying to protect yourself by not allowing people to see your sensitive side?

3. Do you like when people "sm-eyes" at you or does it make you feel uncomfortable?

21 ~ Driving Miss "D"

    I have formed a very unique friendship with someone I have come to admire and respect. I don't know her full story but I do know that she has experienced a deep loss. She made a decision to overcome that loss by starting a blog. Several years ago our blogging paths crossed and we have become dear friends. I have never met her in person. I only refer to her as Hope. She has come to call me "Miss D". I'm pretty sure I'm old enough to be her mother but she has helped me every bit as much as I hope I have helped her. Hope is one talented girl. She is a beautiful poet and writes great stories to share her talent with the world. Every morning in cyberspace, I visit with her. She doesn't know my full story either but for one reason or another our heart-strings are attached. We found each other because it was meant to be, that I know for sure.

    I love the nickname Hope has given me. As you know, my name is **D**olores. Little does Hope know…yet I'm sure she suspects that I have known many other words starting with the letter **D** which have **d**eeply affected me over the years. I know the meaning of **d**iscouragement and **d**isappointment like so many of us have but I also have experienced **d**espair and **d**eep **d**epression. Over thirty years ago, I could hardly convince myself to get out of bed. If it weren't for my young children and the need to get them off to school, I'm not so sure I would have bothered. During those dark times in my life I felt very little hope, if any at all.

I have formed another very unique and precious cyberspace friendship with a woman named Nikki. Nikki and I also communicate on a daily basis. We know a lot more about each other because we have read each other's books and we've had the opportunity apart from the blogging world to share more personal information. Nikki makes my day in much the same way as Hope. She is open and honest. She's had a tough life but she found peace with it by finding her faith. She is a survivor of rape and abuse, both physical and emotional. She has also created a blog to help in her healing process. She has touched my life in such a way that it brings tears to my eyes as I think of her story.

I feel so fortunate to have found such wonderful friends. In the old days, they would be called pen pals. I had one or two of them in my school days but with the technological advances present today, there is no longer the need for paper and pen communication. By reaching out, these two women have honored me in such an indescribable way. We have shared our stories of hope. We have inspired each other in our personal healing journeys. We have learned to trust again and to look on the bright side of things. I personally have found another **D** word which my daughter uses in her writing to describe her relationship with God. I have found the **D**ivine. The One who is all loving and all merciful. The One that loves me no matter what. You know what else? I have discovered several other words beginning with **D** to describe where I am in my journey today. I have encountered a **D**eity that surrounds me with **d**aylight instead of **d**arkness, **d**elight instead of **d**read and **d**espair, and **d**auntless faith instead of **d**eep **d**epression based on irrational fears. I much prefer these words starting with **D** rather than the opposite ones I was previously feeling on a far more regular basis.

Personal Reflections:

1. Have you or do you suffer from some of the same **D** words described in this chapter?
2. If so, do you count on your family and friends to help you rise above your **d**espair, **d**read, or **d**epression?
3. Have you figured out ways to help yourself in order to **d**iscover your faith and **d**elight in the life you have been so richly given?

22 ~ Change

"The best and most beautiful things in the world cannot be seen or even touched. They must be felt with the heart." ~ Helen Keller

As I have already stated several times, I have been married to my husband for over forty-five years. Every night when I pray before I fall asleep, I thank God for this wondrous gift. My husband isn't perfect. Hey…but then, neither am I. However, one of the very first things I am grateful for each and every day and night is our long time marriage and the love and loyalty we share despite the ups and downs of any lifelong commitment. We have experienced financial hardship, job loss, ill physical and emotional health, and other typical marriage woes. Over the years, we have learned the true meaning of our marriage vows. I have discovered that I married my best friend who has stuck by my side through thick and thin. Figuratively speaking…because my husband is not the most demonstrative type of guy, we've held each other's hand as we worked through these trials and tribulations. No one ever said that it was going to be easy but it's been well worth it.

Many years ago when we were in our late teens, my husband's brother tried to influence us not to get married so young. He was eight years older than us and he was offering his younger brother what he thought was some sage advice. Needless to say, we never took it; however, I recall a humorous moment in the first few years of our marriage when my husband showed a little "sass". He mentioned to his brother that "if he had known marriage was going to be this great, he would have gotten married sooner!" So yes...I do have every reason to be grateful for this husband of mine. What about you? Are there things in your life that you are grateful for or don't want to change?

For instance, here is another example of being grateful for the simple things in our lives. Do you have a favorite chair in your home? Do you usually have the tendency to sit in the same kind of chair whenever possible or wherever you go? I know that I do!

When I have the opportunity to visit in other people's homes, one of the first things I do after the initial niceties are out-of-the-way is look for the spot where I am going to sit. I scan the room with hopeful anticipation that I will find a rocking chair or glider rocker. To me, this kind of chair is both comfortable and comforting. In new and awkward situations, when I have the chance to sit on one, it takes the edge off the moment as the rocking motion brings its soothing relief to me.

It is very hard for me to start my day without a short stint on my rocking chair each and every morning. It sets the pace for the whole day as I find my source of peace and contentment in this simplest of ways. It is during this time on my rocking chair that I listen to the softest of music and feel so inspired. This is my time, this is my special spot.

On holidays or visiting with family and friends, I always feel a tiny absence in my life when I'm "off my rocker". I can't be the only one that feels this way. What about you? Do you miss the comfort of your special chair? Are there some things in your life that you just don't want to change?

"You have not found your place until all your faculties are roused, and your whole nature consents and approves of the work you are doing…" ~ Orison Swett Marden

23 ~ Live...Laugh...Love ~ More on a Lighter Note

"In the midst of hate, I found there was, within me, an invincible love. In the midst of tears, I found there was, within me, an invincible smile. In the midst of chaos, I found there was, within me, an invincible calm. I realized, through it all, that in the middle of winter, I finally found that within me there lies an invincible summer." ~ **Albert Camus**

A few years ago, I received an email from my oldest granddaughter. She made me laugh. She was using words like "u" instead of "you" and some of the other shorthand words that young people use today when texting to speed up the process. I remember when she signed off with a colon and a bracket. I had to write her back and ask her what it meant. She told me to look at it by tilting my head to the side and I would see that it was meant to be a smile. Doing just that, actually made me smile. I must admit that I find it so interesting to learn all these new methods of communication. This has encouraged me to make every effort to continue to increase my computer knowledge.

Not too long ago, the only thing I knew how to do was to send or respond to emails and google for information about a subject I wanted to research. I'm still no computer whiz but I'm pretty sure that even my granddaughter would be proud of my progress. The reason I'm mentioning her today is because at the end of an email she sent me, she had signed off with Live…Laugh…Love.

As soon as I saw these closing words, I immediately asked her if she minded if I signed off the same way. She gladly gave me permission and I have utilized this salutation several times when I email my friends or autograph one of my books. Often times, I think of my granddaughter when I do so. Every time I use them in any way, I take the opportunity to ponder upon the true meaning of these three simple little words in hope that the receiver of my message will be richly blessed.

"You will find as you look back upon your life that the moments that stand out, the moments when you have really lived, are the moments when you have done things in the spirit of love." ~ *Henry Drummond*

Now, after all these years I must admit that I am still not a computer whiz. However, I will say this…I am a very determined person. If I don't know something, I ask someone who does. I've plodded along and figured out an awful lot on my own. I've gained confidence and self-esteem in the process.

The other day, my husband came up from his basement office and admitted to me that he can't believe how far I've come in this regard. It is so neat to hear him compliment me this way. He's always had computer skills far greater than mine, but now, once in a while I can actually educate him on a new skill I've learned on my own. I'm grateful for the support and encouragement that I receive so that I can plod on and educate myself in this new and exciting way.

"All things are difficult before they are easy." ~ ***Thomas Fuller***

In the olden days, we could only communicate with those that lived nearby. In this situation, it was from our lips to their ears.

Now with all the advanced technology, one of the best ways to communicate seems to be via computer in one format or another. If it isn't by e-mail, we're logged on to Facebook, Twitter, My Space, chat lines, cell phones, and so on. These methods of communication are all great but have we lost the personal touch? In the future, will we be able to interpret moods, facial expressions, body language, voice intonation, and many other forms of communication, if we choose to mainly communicate the techie way?

Please let us try to remember the personal touch. It's difficult to hug and embrace the "old" way with all the "new" technology. Give someone a smile or a hug today. You'll both feel better for it!

"We cannot rebuild the world ourselves, but we can have a small part in it by beginning where we are. It may only be taking care of a neighbor's child or inviting someone to dinner, but it's important." ~ Donna L. Glazier

24 ~ My Phantom Tooth ~ More on a Lighter Note

"Once you have learned to love, you have learned to live." ~ Source Unknown

Have any of you ever had a root canal? If you have, no fun, right? Many years ago when I was overtired, one of my teeth gave way and I had to go on antibiotics to clear up an abscess and then eventually have a root canal.

The procedure itself wasn't as bad as I thought it would be. What concerned me the most was that the tooth giving me the trouble wasn't a back tooth that could be easily concealed if things didn't go as I hoped. It would be very evident if I lost this tooth.

Over the years, I've had a lot of trouble with this root canal. I had to have it redone about ten years later because it got re-infected. As recently as four years ago it was necessary to have oral surgery to treat it once again. Shortly thereafter, I was forced to have the tooth extracted as the infection reared its ugly head yet again. It seemed that every time I overdid things and let myself get run down this phantom tooth acted up and started to ache. It was almost like a built-in alarm system to remind me to slow down. At last, I'm finally learning how to better listen to this body of mine by being aware of my inner signal, my phantom tooth.

We all have inner guidelines to help us not overdo. Mine just happens to be my missing tooth which somehow or other, can still ache. My dentist tells me that there is now a weakness in this area where a healthy tooth once existed. According to him, this is why I have phantom toothaches.

"Health, Learning & Virtue will ensure your happiness; they will give you a quiet conscience, private esteem & public honor." ~ Thomas Jefferson

Personal Reflections:

1. What is your weakness and how does it manifest itself?
2. What is it trying to tell you?
3. I'm slowly learning to listen to my body. It doesn't mean that I always like what it has to say but I know I should obey. When I don't, I'm the one who pays the price in the end. Can you relate to this?

25 ~ Common Courtesy

"We find greatest joy, not in getting, but in expressing what we are...Men do not really live for honors or for pay; their gladness is not in the taking and holding, but in the doing, the striving, the building, the living. It is a higher joy to teach than to be taught. It is good to get justice, but better to do it; fun to have things but more to make them. The happy man is he who lives the life of love, not for the honors it may bring, but for life itself." ~ R. J. Baughan

"Courteous people learn courtesy from the discourteous." ~ Laura Fitzgerald

Does this quote from the book *Veil of Roses* by Laura Fitzgerald ring a bell with you or make any sense to you? It sure does to me. Common courtesy or common decency can be as uncommon as common sense. As you can see, I'm full of oxymorons as I take the opportunity to elaborate on this subject. What I am actually trying to say is this...when I witness people being rude or unkind to others, it really gets my goat. As soon as I observe such unacceptable behavior I always do a self-check. Subsequently, I almost bend over backwards to treat people with even more kindness than I normally do.

There is no way that I want to behave in such a discourteous or disrespectful manner. In essence, I immediately become even more courteous and behave the exact opposite of the negative behavior that I may have just observed. Therefore, the above quote may actually be true in many instances. If people are discourteous in your presence, it may have a positive impact on your future behavior. My husband and I have a couple of cute expressions of our own. When we observe bad behavior my husband will often say…"if I ever act like that, please let me know" or "remind me 'not' to act in such a rude manner". What do you think? Do you also bend over backwards to 'not' act the same discourteous way that you may have witnessed?

I had a very rewarding conversation with one of my daughters a few years ago. At the end of the school year, my granddaughters were receiving their final report cards. This was an especially important end-of-the-year ceremony because they were in the process of moving to another city during the summer. My two oldest granddaughters were fifteen and twelve at the time and it created a period of adjustment for them. Although, my daughter realized that there would be a transition period, she had every reason to be optimistic. Both girls were doing well in school and had received academic awards in the past. At the finale of this particular year-end ceremonies, the younger granddaughter received this very unique award. It was titled the **WWJD** Award.

I reacted the very same way as my daughter did when she first heard the news that Becca was to receive this special award. I quickly asked, "What in the world does **WWJD** stand for"? This was her reply…"It stands for the "**W**hat **W**ould **J**esus **D**o" Award if He were in your shoes.

In essence, my granddaughter's classmates had nominated her for the award in recognition of the most Christ-like behavior observed by them in her interactions with her peer group. That sounds like a fine compliment to me. Wouldn't it be wonderful if our behavior emulated Christ's as well in our dealings with our own peer group?

On a similar note, sometime ago, my then two-year old granddaughter told me that I was her best friend. Wow…where does a two-year old hear such an expression? Well, she has three older siblings and I'm sure she heard it from one of them when they were talking either with or about their friends.

I was very touched when she made this comment, although, I'm not so sure she knew exactly what she was saying. Young children, usually go to great lengths and have much need for a best friend. It's all part of the growing up process. I'm pretty sure we have all been there.

As the years have gone by, I've come to realize that my younger girlish need for a best friend no longer exists. My best friend is my husband and all my female and male friends are just that, my friends. I love them, enjoy them, and I relish the relationships that we share.

Over the years as part of the maturation process, I have changed my focus. For many years now, my goal in life has been "to be" a best friend rather than "to have" a best friend based on some insecure need of mine. By doing so, I hope my aspiration of emulating my granddaughter in her **WWJD** behavior shines out as much as humanly possible. I have surrounded myself with a wonderful group of people, both female and male. I always try my best to be a true and loyal friend. I have every desire to take their feelings into consideration at every opportunity. Hopefully, one day my young granddaughter will realize that I am truly her best friend because I love her with all my heart. Isn't that what being a best friend is really all about? I sure hope so because my friends mean the world to me.

As I continue on this lighter note, I would like to add that I try to view life in the simplest of ways and to use my imagination as much as possible to explain my thoughts. This is the reason I use my personal experiences to make a variety of points. It is necessary for me to draw from this wealth of information in order to urge you to tap into your past and find the correlation between your life and what I am trying to say. This gives my readers a better chance of relating to my message and how it might apply in their own lives.

Here's another example of tapping into your imagination. Our lives can be as plain and simple as two slices of bread stuck together with butter or as exciting as the ingredients that we put into it. I much prefer what is between the slices of bread rather than the bread itself, although, I do enjoy good quality bread. In reality, I need both.

I want my sandwich so thick with meat and other fixings so that I can hardly wrap my mouth around it. This is the same way that I want to enjoy my life. I don't just want to be born and then eventually die. That's a given. In other words, I don't merely want to exist. I want a lot of in-between stuff to make a really good life for myself and for those around me.

I can settle for bread squeezed together with butter or margarine or I can have a huge "Dagwood" sandwich with all of my favorite things in the middle. It's up to me. As I said, I can settle for less or build my life in much the same way that

I make my sandwiches, thick with messy and juicy flavors like pickles and peppers. I want to lead a full and rewarding life that is pleasing to my Maker. How about you? Would you be a possible candidate for the **WWJD** Award?

26 ~ What's Eating Gilbert Grape?

"An obvious fact about negative feelings is often overlooked. They are caused by us, not by exterior happenings. An outside event presents the challenge, but we react to it. So we must attend to the way we take things, not to the things themselves." ~ Vernon Howard

My daughter uses a neat expression when she notices that someone doesn't appear to be up to snuff or in a particularly good mood. She will say, "I wonder what's eating Gilbert Grape!" Sometimes I feel like Gilbert Grape myself. For whatever reason, I occasionally get set off by the negative behavior of others just like we all do. I am going to explain one of my pet peeves to you. Maybe it's one of yours too.

First of all I want to start by asking a question. In your opinion, is there such a concept as "reasonable" expectations? If not, this chapter probably does not apply to...if so, please read on. At times, I get frustrated by what appears to be a lack of response or reaction to a request I've made or a question I've asked. Let me put it another way. Am I being unreasonable if I ask a question and expect an answer? I will give you a few other examples of what I mean even if they don't all apply to you just so that you get a better understanding of the point I am trying to make. Some may apply while others may not. These are simply yes and no types of questions...

If someone gives you their word...is it reasonable to expect them to keep it?

If you send an email asking a question or questions ...is it reasonable to expect a response?

If you leave a message on someone's answering machine...is it reasonable to expect them to return your call?

If you celebrate a person's birthday with a card, gift, or treat them to lunch...is it reasonable to expect them to acknowledge your birthday in some way, shape, or form?

If you have gone out of your way to help a person out (i.e. by helping them move for instance)....is it reasonable to expect that they might return a similar favor one day should you require their help?

When a friend's been sick and you've supported them by sending cards or gifts...is it reasonable to think they might wish you well when you're ill or at least call to see how you are doing?

These are just examples of a few possible questions I am using in order to make my point. I would love to know if you can identify with it. Do you ever have "reasonable" expectations? Or in other words, are you disappointed when others don't react the way you think they might considering the friendship you have or the relationship you might have formed? If so…does that mean it is wrong to feel the way you do?

I am making every effort to have fewer expectations of people. Trust me, this is no easy endeavor. I am working very hard to turn that occasional sour grape attitude of mine into a reason to celebrate. I am also making every effort to dwell on the positives in my life and be grateful for all my blessings. We all have bad days when people turn us off and we get these negative emotions that certainly don't make us feel any better about the person or the situation.

What can we do about it? We can change our own attitudes just like it was stated in the previous quote by Vernon Howard and not fall into the negative claptrap. It is not easy to be in a positive frame of mind all of the time but when we work at it, it can really make a big difference. Most of us have heard the adage about being handed a lemon in life and turning it into lemonade. Well, we all know what we can turn grapes into…right? Celebrate the good things in your life and more good things will come your way. Cheers to you all!

Personal Reflections:

1. Is it okay to have "reasonable" expectations of others? If so, why? If not, why? Please Note: There are pros and cons to both answers. Do you know what they are?
2. Is it okay to admit to yourself that someone's behavior has negatively affected you?
3. When a family member or friend is not there for you when you've been there for them in the past, how do you react?
4. Do you have the ability and wherewithal to turn the situation around and respond in a positive manner?

27 ~ Self-Acceptance and Regrets

How many of us live without regrets? No one...I am sure! How many of us repeat the same mistakes over and over again? If we don't learn from our mistakes, this is exactly what we will do. Often times, I will ask myself the rhetorical question of why a certain situation arises over and over again in my life. My daughter's answer is that I didn't learn my lesson the first time around.

When history repeats itself, even if the players are different, I try to remember my daughter's sage words. When a similar situation keeps revisiting me, I have no choice but to acknowledge and accept that there is a life lesson in it for me. It's up to me to figure out what it is and perhaps I will have fewer regrets and more learning power. The gift of wisdom...it can be so elusive.

"Never mistake knowledge for wisdom. One helps you make a living; the other helps you make a life." ~ Sandra Carey

Isn't it strange how we meet many people in life who appear to be so self-confident and poised? Perhaps those who genuinely are, have no need to read motivational books like mine. Maybe, you are one of these fortunate people but the fact that you are at the final stages of reading my book leads me to believe that you might be relating to some of my observations and insights. Many of us are able to project an aura or image that implies that we are more confident than we may actually be.

For those of you who may, at times, feel inadequate, insecure, know the meaning of fear, failure, and human weakness, then perhaps some of what I have to share may very well appeal to you. I sure hope so because this has been my goal all along. I want to reach out and touch people in such an intimate way in order to make a difference in their lives.

Part of this goal is to reassure you that you are not alone and it is okay to be human. We are not all cut from the same cloth and we must make the best of the gifts that we have been so generously given. In my opinion, it is wiser to deal with negative feelings in order to help overcome them so as to better cope with life rather than bury them deep within ourselves. When we suppress our true emotions, sooner or later, they come back to haunt us. Self-acceptance is the key. Although we are equally loved by our Maker, for reasons unknown to us, we are not all equally endowed.

Some stars in the heavenly sky are bigger and brighter than other ones just like the personalities and varied talents of people. When the smaller stars join together they can create the same dazzling effect as some of the larger ones. Some of us need to surround ourselves with like-minded people in order to shine brighter. It's just the way it is. Whether big or small, we all draw our Light from the same Divine Source.

Those of us that may not have the success, confidence, intelligence, good looks, poise etc., that we might desire can benefit from combining what we have to offer with others. In doing so, we can creatively connect to each other to develop our own Milky Way effect. When shining this way we have agreed to cast the light on others in this wonderful and generous way by lighting up the lives of others while simultaneously lighting up our own lives. No candle ever goes out when it lights up another one. It merely succeeds in sharing its fire. It's up to us to share the limelight so that each of us has the opportunity to showcase our talents.

Personal Reflections:

1. Do you like to be in the limelight or the center of attention?
2. If so why? Is it really because you are secure in who you are or in actuality is it the exact opposite?
3. If you prefer to be on the sidelines, do you consider this to be a character flaw? If so, why?

4. Not all personalities like to draw attention to themselves. I've asked this question before, do you consider yourself to be an introvert or an extrovert?

5. Do you accept yourself for whom you are or do you secretly wish you were more like someone else? Please Note: It is okay to want to emulate others but it is also necessary to positively embrace our own personalities. There is no benefit in coveting another person's life and being dissatisfied with our own.

28 ~ And the Winner is...Not Me!

One of my husband's favorite lines is, "it's hard to fly like an eagle when you're surrounded by a bunch of turkeys". ~ Source Unknown

I previously mentioned in one of my other chapters, The Weather Channel, that my husband should consider being a sit-down-comedian. He certainly has the makings of one as he comes up with some pretty humorous comments from what appears to be an endless supply of quips. In jest, he used to say the above quote quite often during his working years to express his frustration when dealing with the shortcomings of people. I can't help but wonder what they were saying about him.

After publishing my first book, my husband persuaded me to enter a book writing contest. My initial response was "no way". First of all, I never realized that you had to actually submit a fee to enter this particular contest and possibly other ones as well. There were other necessary procedures and requirements that were needed along with this submission entry fee. Up to this point, I was naïve enough to think that people actually nominated authors to be selected as a potential winners in writing contests based on the pleasure they found in reading their books. It never entered my mind that writers paid a fee to submit their own books. Also the other reason I was reluctant to enter this contest is that I only had one book under my belt and I knew there was a lot of room for improvement. My husband rationalized that if I didn't enter then there was no way I could win. Therefore, even if it was a long shot I entered the contest with major reservations and against my better judgment. Internally, I didn't want the negative feelings of realizing that my book wasn't up to par.

You guessed it! I did not win.

Since then, I have heard and read several comments to the effect that merely having written a book makes us all winners. It has been said that there were no losers in this contest because we have accomplished a great feat by having the courage to enter our books in the contest. Well, yes and no. This rationalization does not totally make sense or even appeal to me. It sounds more like an appeasement. Why enter a contest in the first place if there is no honor or reward in winning it? If we are all winners even if we lose, than maybe the reverse is true and the winners are losers too just like the rest of us.

Whoever said, 'It's not whether you win or lose that counts,' probably lost." ~ Martina Navratilova

I'm Not Perfect And It's Okay is written in an imperfect way much like its author, me. I'm sorry to admit that there are a few typos in it that my editor, my proofreaders and I missed. Oops...I guess they are not perfect either. I heard an expression just the other day. It was about being "beautifully imperfect". I've now made that my own personal goal, to be beautiful despite my imperfections.

However, in the end, it is my name on my book and I am ultimately responsible for its content. I wouldn't have it any other way. Yes, maybe it is not as well-written or as polished as some other books, but what the heck; I gave it my best shot. The negative consequence of not winning the contest will not deter me. It will only suffice to make me more determined. I'm like a dog with a bone and I'm not going to give up that easy.

Although, I will say this...no matter how hard anyone may try to flower up the facts, to be brutally honest, along with many other authors...I lost and some other authors won. That's a fact. Contests are actually competitions. In most, if not all competitive events, there are winners and losers. Usually, there are far more losers than winners. I will not take that honor away from the winners. By saying that we are all winners in this book writing contest does just that...it takes away from the winners. I lost, I know it, and I'm not afraid to admit it. I'm not afraid to admit this either. It mattered...in fact, it mattered a lot more than I thought it would. I have a competitive spirit and it's no fun to lose. I'm sure that it mattered to the winners too. If it didn't, why would any of us enter contests in the first place?

Therefore, on that note I would like to congratulate all the winners in, not only writing contests, but in other competitive events as well. It feels so wonderful to win and hopefully one day the rest of us will win a contest too. There is nothing wrong with being a gracious loser or gracious winner for that matter either.

"Do not go where the path may lead you, go instead where there is no path and leave a trail." ~ *Ralph Waldo Emerson*

This is a very profound quote. If I can leave anything with you today, I would like to give you the gift of believing in yourself. It won't happen in one day, but maybe it will be the first seed that when nurtured, will bloom into a very fruitful tree. So many of us look for validation outside of ourselves to identify who we are by how others react to us. We may look to others for approval instead of being our authentic self. It is necessary to find that validation from within in order to have a true belief in ourselves.

If we rely on others to form this belief, we may lose sight of all that we hope to be because we have compromised facets of our own personality and character so that we will be loved and accepted. This is conditional love. It takes real courage and true grit to be different and stand up for our beliefs. We can only find this courage when we have the strength and determination to validate who we are from the inner stirrings of our Maker.

Although, these stirrings may begin by a dissatisfaction or lack of contentment in our lives that just won't leave us, there is a reason for this. If we are always satisfied with our situation in life, there would be no room for growth or any desire to change our circumstances or anyone else's for that matter. Growth results in many fine attributes like self-worth, self-esteem, and a desire to make a difference. With these attributes, we learn about hope and the gift of believing in ourselves…a gift so wondrous that we can stand tall and be exactly whom we were meant to be regardless of other people's opinion of us.

Be true to these inner stirrings and you will learn how to believe in yourself.

When I look at all the great authors in my writing and reading path, I know that I am in great company. I feel like I am soaring with eagles and not "surrounded by a bunch of turkeys". We are a bunch of gifted writers making a difference by sharing our God-given talents.

"Achievement is not always success, while reputed failure often is. It is honest endeavor, persistent effort to do the best possible under any and all circumstances." ~ Orison Swett Marden

Personal Reflections:

1. Do you ever enter contests? If so what kind and do you hope to win?
2. Do you enter personal ones that have the opportunity to evaluate your talent?
3. If you don't win, how do you feel about it?
4. If you do win, does it make sense to you if someone says...everyone is a winner in this contest just because they entered it? Four of my grandchildren play hockey and some of the other grandchildren play different sports. When anyone of them loses their game, even at their young age, I have yet to hear them say that even though they lost the game..."they still won".

29 ~ Extraordinarily Ordinary

"There are no great people in this world, only great challenges which ordinary people rise up to meet." ~ William Frederick Halsy, Jr.

Over forty years ago, my niece Lori was born. When she came into this world, it was a milestone birth for me because I was given the first-time honor of becoming a Godmother to this lovely little baby. In most instances, one might consider being a Godparent as a pretty ordinary thing but to me it was really quite extraordinary. In my day, it usually meant that if the parents were unable to care for the child, the Godparent would be willing to take on this huge responsibility in the parent's absence. Nowadays, I'm pretty sure most parents have guardians named in their Wills if the need should arise but I'm not so sure that was as prevalent in my younger years, at least not to my knowledge. We took a lot more for granted and had the tendency to assume that our children would be taken care of by our chosen family members if the unthinkable should happen.

We later honored our siblings in much the same way when our children were born. We chose carefully in order to ensure that if the need ever arose, our children would be loved and provided for in much the same way as we would raise them ourselves.

As the years went by we were given the honor of becoming Godparents on more than one occasion. Each and every time it felt like such an extraordinary event. It was always a great honor to be selected. Now all these years later, although we don't have the same initial responsibility of taking over for the parents if need be, I feel we still have the responsibility of setting an example for these wonderful Godchildren. This makes our role in their lives still extraordinary even to this day. I'm grateful to have had this opportunity and to be honored in this way.

"Each time the world needs an extra touch of love and gentle caring, God creates a Godmother." ~ Source Unknown

30 ~ Savor the Flavor

I received a lovely Christmas present from a gentleman in his mid-seventies whom I hardly know. He is actually a dear and longtime friend of my sister.

I feel that a great gift has been bestowed upon me at this later stage of my life in what I refer to as the beginning of my twilight years. After completion of my first book *I'm Not Perfect and It's Okay*, I found such wonderful support from my husband, my family and my friends. This, too, felt like a generous gift which created that Christmas feeling all year long.

The gentleman I mentioned earlier became a fan of mine shortly after he read my first book. On completion of reading it, he demonstrated a keen desire to read more. He eagerly accepted to read the manuscript for my second book. Are you like me? Do you like immediate feedback? Do you patiently wait to hear or read the reactions of others to what you have so carefully written? Our words are so important to us because they are an expression of our innermost self that we are choosing to share with others. This choice involves risk. I feel I show my faith the most when I am prepared to take that risk. By choosing to share my words with you today

I am taking a small step in my life journey in order to grow in faith.

On Christmas Eve, shortly before my sister's friend was to attend Midnight Mass, he gave me the most incredible Christmas gift. I had sent him my second manuscript a few weeks earlier and was waiting patiently to get some feedback. He wrote that he was reading the chapter titled God's Wife and he was so moved by it that he decided to immediately e-mail me. He mentioned that he was reading my manuscript much like he was enjoying Christmas candy. He was reading slowly to better absorb and digest my words and their meaning. He said that he was enjoying what I had written in the way that I meant it to be read…slowly, very slowly, one chapter at a time to "savor the flavor".

I think that is an excellent expression to describe my inspirational books and the Christmas Season as well. The true meaning of Christmas is meant to be savored all year long because it is the gift that keeps on giving. Savor the flavor…sounds like a fine compliment to me. What wonderful gifts God has in store for us all! It is so enchanting to discover a new talent later on in life. It means we still have room for growth and more opportunities to reveal our hidden talents.

Personal Reflections:

1. Do you consider yourself to be a talented person?
2. If so, do you think you have discovered all your talents or are you open to uncovering some latent possibilities?
3. Have you tapped into to any other resources to help zero in on your creative abilities in another direction?

Conclusion

I have learned that success is to be measured not so much by the position one has reached in life as by the obstacles which he has overcome in trying to succeed." ~ Booker T. Washington

The majority of my writing is faith-based and I draw from my own personal inspiration and relationship with God. I don't know the plan. All I know is that I am...as are you, part of the Divine Plan which is far greater than anyone of us could possibly imagine. If things don't go quite as we expect or see fit, it doesn't mean to say that all won't turn out for the better. Miracles take time.

Often times, life can appear magical but miracles don't happen quite as quickly. We must exercise extreme patience and diligence in order for our own personal plan to unfold. God is not in a hurry nor should we be.

"The sculptor will chip off all unnecessary material to set the angel free. Nature will chip and pound us remorselessly to bring out our possibilities. She will strip us of wealth, humble our pride, humiliate our ambition, let us down from the ladder of fame, will discipline us in a

thousand ways, if she can develop a little character. Everything must give way to that. Wealth is nothing, position is nothing, fame is nothing, and manhood is everything." ~ *Orison Swett Marden*

Good things can and do happen to good people. God has promised us many things and He is true to His Word. We must count on that in our daily lives.

"Each experience through which we pass operates ultimately for our good...This is a correct attitude to adopt...and we must be able to see it in that light." ~ *Raymond Holliwell*

We don't always recognize the work of God, but if we are patient with ourselves and take the time to reflect, we will create the opportunity to see exactly how God works. When we do, we will be forever grateful and recognize how truly blessed we are.

OTHER BOOKS
AVAILABLE BY
AUTHOR DOLORES AYOTTE

I'M NOT PERFECT AND IT'S OKAY
~ Thirteen Steps to a Happier Self ~

GROWING UP AND LIKING IT
~ More Steps to a Happier Self ~

UP THE "DOWN" LADDER
~ Simple Ideas to Overcome Depression ~

TO CONTACT AUTHOR:

WEBSITE

http://www.doloresayotte.com

BLOG SITE

http://www.doloresayotte.wordpress.com

FACEBOOK AUTHOR'S PAGE

http://www.facebook.com/Author.Dolores.Ayotte

Made in the USA
Charleston, SC
02 August 2016